MILK AND HONEY

A Comedy

by

PHILIP KING

GW00707392

SAMUEL FRENCH

LONDON
NEW YORK   SYDNEY   TORONTO   HOLLYWOOD

MILK AND HONEY

Produced by the Worthing Theatre Company
at the Connaught Theatre, Worthing, on 13 July 1959
with the following cast of characters—

(in order of their appearance)

BARBARA MARTIN Joan Sims
BASIL MARTIN Roland Curram
GEORGE PADSTOW Michael Lees
DELIA BROWN Jill Hyem
THE MILKMAN Richard Clarke
FAITH BRANTINGHAM Grazina Frame

The play directed by GUY VAESEN
Setting by Robert Weaver

SYNOPSIS OF SCENES

The action of the play passes in the living-room and kitchen of
the Martin's house on the outskirts of Brighton

ACT I
Saturday morning—7.30 a.m.

ACT II
SCENE 1 Mid-morning, the same day
SCENE 2 Half-an-hour later

ACT III
12.40 p.m. the same day

Time—the present

ACT I

Scene—*The living-room and kitchen of the Martins' house on the outskirts of Brighton. 7.30 a.m. in late summer.*

The living-room is stage L *and the kitchen* R. *Both rooms are very modern—tastefully but not expensively furnished. The living-room has an archway* C *leading to the hall, and a door in the dividing wall leading to the kitchen. The staircase can just be seen in the hall. Large french windows up* L *lead to the garden. The fireplace, with an electric fire, is down* L. *The kitchen has a door leading to the rear of the house in the down* R *corner of the back wall. The kitchen window is* L *of the door, and has a sink and cooker below it. If it is impracticable to show these they could be set behind a screen, behind which* BARBARA *might go when important dialogue is going on in the living-room.*

When the CURTAIN *rises, the window-curtains in the living-room are closed and the room is in semi-darkness.* BARBARA MARTIN *is in the kitchen. She is a pleasant-faced housewife of around thirty—a normal, happy woman. Her fault, if it is a fault, is that she is too house-proud. She wears a working housecoat. She is setting out cups and saucers—two on a tray, two on the kitchen table. She puts the kettle on the stove and lights it. Then she places a small sugar-bowl on the tray, and gets the tea-pot and tea ready for when the kettle has boiled. She then moves into the living-room, draws the curtains and looks round the room. Her face at once registers disapproval. The room is by no means in a chaotic state, but there are full ashtrays about, rumpled newspapers, three empty glasses and one or two bottles, and cushions on chairs and the settee which have obviously not been shaken, and there are other signs of a room left untouched after an evening's use.*

BARBARA (*annoyed*) T' t' t'. (*She goes to the settee and begins to shake the cushions*)

(*The kettle whistle sounds*)

(*With a start*) Oh, my goodness! (*She goes to the kitchen and proceeds to make the tea*)

(BASIL MARTIN, *her husband, comes down the stairs into the living-room. He is a year or so older than Barbara, good-looking and of a cheerful disposition. He is in pyjamas and dressing-gown. He looks around the room and is at once conscience-stricken about its untidiness*)

BASIL (*quietly, but in a near-to-panic voice*) Oh, Lord! (*He looks swiftly towards the kitchen door, then immediately bustles around "tidying". He begins by "plumping" cushions madly in the armchair* L)

(BARBARA *hears him and comes into doorway from kitchen*)

BARBARA (*firmly*) You're too late! I've seen it!

BASIL (*spinning round to face her*) Oh Lord!

BARBARA. Basil Martin, what was the last thing I said to you before I went to bed?

BASIL (*moving* C, *quoting*) "Put the cat out and tidy the room."

BARBARA (*crossing to the fireplace, heavily*) But you didn't, did you?

BASIL (*muttering*) I put the cat out!

BARBARA. But this room! Basil, really! It's too bad of you.

BASIL. I'm sorry, darling, honestly I am. But old George was yarning on, and somehow I just forgot about the room. (*Hopefully trying to change the subject*) Er—is there a cup of tea going? (*He moves towards the kitchen*)

BARBARA (*moving past him into the kitchen*) You know very well there is. (*She goes to the table and begins to pour out tea into the cups on the tray*)

BASIL (*coming into the kitchen to* L *of her—with overdone heartiness*) Good old Babs! (*He rubs his hands vigorously as he says this, then catches Barbara's eyes and sobers up considerably*)

BARBARA (*looking at his hair*) Why *must* you always look like a Hottentot in the early morning?

BASIL. Hottentot?

BARBARA. Or a Skiffle Grouper. Your hair! Would it be asking too much of you to run a comb through it?

BASIL. I—I'll do it right away. Anything to make you happy, darling!

BARBARA (*with a look at him*) Are you feeling lightheaded? (*Referring to the tea*) You'd better take George and Delia theirs first.

BASIL (*starting*) Er—Delia's? You—you want me to take hers too?

BARBARA. Why not?

BASIL. You mean—right into her bedroom?

BARBARA. Good heavens! Why shouldn't you? Even Delia won't expect you to leap into bed with her.

BASIL. I should hope not—with her fiancé in the next room.

BARBARA (*with a look at him*) To say nothing of your wife downstairs.

BASIL. Er—quite!

BARBARA (*handing him the tray*) Off you go. (*Then with a half-smile*) And if you're not down in two minutes I shall be up those stairs like a shot from a gun!

BASIL (*kissing her hair*) Darling! (*Looking at the cups on the tray*) Which is which?

BARBARA. It doesn't matter. Neither of them are sugared. Oh, and tell them not to get up yet. The place will have to be straightened before they come down. That room—(*with a jerk of her head*)—looks like a four ale bar. (*With a "shooing" gesture*) Go on—before it's stone cold!

(BASIL *goes through into the living-room.* BARBARA *pours herself a cup of tea. As* BASIL *is passing through living-room he picks up a crumpled cushion from the settee with one hand and shakes it vigorously, returns it to the settee and goes into the hall and upstairs.*

BARBARA, *having taken a sip of tea, quickly puts cup down and runs through the living-room and out into the hall)*

BARBARA (*calling*) Basil!
BASIL (*off*) Good Lord! I've only reached the top of the stairs.
BARBARA (*calling*) Ask them about breakfast.
BASIL. Oh! (*Calling*) 'Morning, George, old man! Can I come in.

(*The hearty voice of* GEORGE PADSTOW *is heard answering*)

GEORGE (*off*) Yes, rather! 'Morning, Bas, old boy!
BARBARA (*coming back into the living-room, muttering as she does so*) "George old man. Bas old boy". (*She automatically shakes a cushion on the settee—the same one that Basil shook—as she goes back into the kitchen and drinks more tea, then pours out a cup for Basil. Muttering*) What a life! (*She sits on the stool*)

(BASIL *comes downstairs into the living-room and through into the kitchen*)

BASIL (*nervously—and not knowing quite what else to say*) Er—hello! (*He crosses to* R *of Barbara*)
BARBARA (*after a look at him—heavily*) Hello. And *what?*
BASIL (*blinking*) What, what?
BARBARA. What is it you want to say, but daren't?
BASIL (*airily*) Oh, it's nothing—except—(*not airily*)—they're getting up right away.
BARBARA. What? (*Rising*) But I told you to tell them . . .
BASIL. I know, darling, but old George says it's such a lovely morning—and—and—well they're getting up right away.
BARBARA (*sitting on the table, downstage corner*) Well, if they think that breakfast will be ready—did you ask them about breakfast, by the way?
BASIL (*gulping*) Er—yes. Darling—George says he doesn't want *anything* . . .
BARBARA. Good!
BASIL (*continuing*) . . . anything in the way of cereals. Just bacon and eggs or sausages or—well, you know.
BARBARA (*rising and taking her cup to the sink, heavily*) Yes, I know. (*Going to the fridge or cupboard down* R) Cooked breakfast for one!
BASIL (*muttering*) Oh, and Delia says that actually, although she doesn't usually—she wouldn't mind . . .
BARBARA (*heavily*) Cooked breakfast for two!
BASIL (*moving to the stool, hedging*) Well—Babs—as you're cooking for them—I thought . . . (*He sits on the stool*)
BARBARA. Cooked breakfast for three! (*Heavily*) Whoopee! Let's

have a party! And three cheers for good old Babs! (*She slams some bacon and sausages down on the table*)

BASIL (*hesitantly, pointing to the cup of tea*) Er—is this mine?

BARBARA. It is—and I hope it chokes you!

BASIL. Oh, come now, old girl . . .

BARBARA. Basil Martin, the next time you invite one of your old Fourth Form buddies and his girl-friend to come and stay with you, please give me decent warning and I'll make it convenient—to be away!

BASIL. But, Babs, I've *told* you, I didn't actually *invite* them. I happened to run into old George in London yesterday, and he told me that he and Delia had fixed to come down to Brighton for a few days, and then suddenly—at the last moment—the people they were going to stay with had let them down.

BARBARA (*heavily*) Had they accidentally met Delia?

BASIL (*exasperated*) I don't know whether they had or not. Anyway . . .

BARBARA (*heavily*) I expect they had!

BASIL (*continuing*) . . . poor old George looked so down in the mouth. He'd tried every reasonable hotel in the town—not a hope of course. Well, Babs—darling—*knowing* that we had room here . . .

BARBARA. And *knowing* that *you* wouldn't have to run after them! (*Stroking his hair back*) Go on—darling . . .!

BASIL. Well, hang it all, I do owe a great deal to old George.

BARBARA (*flatly*) What exactly?

BASIL. My life!

BARBARA (*derisively*) Oh, *that*! (*She moves to the dresser drawers for scissors, a fork, and a board*)

BASIL. If it hadn't been for George I shouldn't be here at this moment.

BARBARA. And I have to cook him a breakfast!

BASIL. If he hadn't fished me out of that pond . . .

BARBARA (*moving back to the table*) He got a medal for it, didn't he?

BASIL. Yes, but . . .

BARBARA. Well then . . . ! (*She stabs a sausage fiercely with the fork*)

BASIL (*wheedling*) Look, darling—I admit I shouldn't have invited them here without consulting you—first . . .

BARBARA (*still stabbing sausages*) You're right. You shouldn't!

BASIL (*suddenly snapping*) But, dammit, I *did* 'phone you!

BARBARA (*also flaring up*) Yes! To *ask* me if they could come, and when I said they couldn't, to *tell* me that you'd already invited them and they were coming!

BASIL (*muttering*) Anyway, they gave me a lift back in their car.

BARBARA (*cutting the sausages one by one*) Very helpful—seeing that you had a day return ticket!

BASIL (*feebly pawing the air*) Look—they'll only be here for a few days . . .

BARBARA (*practically*) How few?

BASIL (*hesitantly*) How—er . . . ?

BARBARA. Few!

BASIL (*nervously*) Well—old George has only got—a fortnight.

BARBARA (*it is almost a yelp*) A *fortnight*! (*She spears a sausage unconsciously*)

BASIL (*terrified*) Sssh! (*He rises to R of her*) They'll hear you! (*Then very quickly*) Could I have another cup of tea? I—I always feel better after another cup of tea. (*He pours himself a cup*)

BARBARA (*pointing the fork plus a sausage at him; threateningly*) Basil Martin, are you telling me . . . (*She realizes she is pointing a sausage at Basil, and impatiently flings the fork on to the table*) A *few* days!

BASIL (*muttering*) Well—er—fourteen. What's that out of a lifetime?

BARBARA (*shortly*) A *lifetime*!

BASIL (*weakly*) Fourteen little days . . .

BARBARA (*unable to believe her ears*) You dare say that to me! You *dare* say that—after what you said when I suggested that we went off somewhere for a *week*—seven little days!

BASIL (*pointing towards the hall and speaking in a hoarse whisper*) Darling—quietly—just between our two selves, eh?

BARBARA. I asked you if we couldn't go away for only a week—this *coming* week, but—oh, no! You'd just got an idea for a new book; you were inspired! You had to strike while the iron was hot! You couldn't spare the time! *Tempus Fugit*, you blathered! (*She starts cutting the rind off the bacon*)

BASIL (*weakly*) Babs . . .

BARBARA. Well, I'm sorry for the "fugit-ing" it will do this next fortnight with—(*pointing*)—those two in the house. It will pass like a prison sentence as far as I'm concerned—and you too! (*With meaning*) I'll see to that! (*She drops the bacon and moves below him to the fridge*)

BASIL. Oh, Lord! (*Desperately*) Babs—it wasn't merely the time I couldn't spare—it was the cash as well. If—or when, my play is put on, and if it's a success . . .

BARBARA (*handing him two eggs*) And *if* we're both not in bathchairs by then!

BASIL. Yes—I mean no . . . If it's a success we can have a dozen holidays. (*He puts the eggs on the table*)

BARBARA. I don't want a dozen holidays, I'll settle for one.

BASIL. I know, my darling, but we just can't afford one this year.

BARBARA (*moving to Basil; weighing every word*) We can't afford a holiday and *yet*—we can afford to house and feed two perfect strangers for fourteen days!

BASIL. They're *not* perfect strangers.

BARBARA. They're certainly not perfect! (*Getting the frying-pan from the cupboard under the sink*) And how long is it since you last clapped eyes on George Padstow.

BASIL (*picking up his cup*) Not since he was expelled from school.

BARBARA. Since he was . . . ? My Lord! Basil Martin, what *have* you brought to the house?

BASIL (*hastily*) It was nothing—really. Boys will be boys, you know, and old George always was one for his little bit of fun.

BARBARA (*grimly*) I can believe that! (*She puts the pan on the stove*) And are you *quite* sure he hasn't brought it down here with him—his "little bit of fun"?

BASIL (*starting*) You mean . . . ?

BARBARA (*nodding*) Delia—yes! (*She takes the fat out of the fridge*)

BASIL (*horrified*) Babs, really! Dammit, they're engaged!

BARBARA. How do you know?

BASIL. George said so. Besides she's wearing an engagement ring!

BARBARA (*weakly*) Go away. Go away before I hit you! If you want your bath you'd better get it *now*. You know our boiler only holds enough for two baths—and it isn't working properly.

BASIL. O.K.! (*He puts his cup and saucer down on the table*)

BARBARA (*sharply*) That doesn't go there! (*She puts the fat in the pan*)

BASIL (*after giving an exasperated look*) No, darling. (*He puts it on the draining board of the sink*) Er—Babs . . . ?

BARBARA (*she is—at all times—busy; putting bacon and sausages into the frying-pan and getting crockery, etc on to a tray on the dresser and preparing breakfast generally*) Well?

BASIL. You—er—you will be—nice to them—George and Delia, won't you?

BARBARA. "Nice"?

BASIL. Well—you weren't too amiable when they arrived last night, were you? You cleared off to bed before they'd been here ten minutes.

BARBARA. After slaving around this house from seven a.m. I am not at my best at eleven forty-five *p.m.*

BASIL (*moving R and muttering*) Yes, I suppose it was rather late . . .

BARBARA. That's an understatement, if ever I heard one—particularly as you'd *told* me on the phone to have a snack ready for you all at eight!

BASIL. Well, you see—I was counting on a straight run down, but old George . . .

BARBARA. I shouldn't think "old George" has ever done anything straight from the day his unfortunate mother got him out of her system!

BASIL (*shocked*) I say, Babs, that's a bit crude, isn't it?

BARBARA (*slamming plates on the tray*) I feel crude! (*She takes the tray to the table*) Which pubs did you stop at on the way down? Or perhaps it would save time if you told me the ones you passed!

BASIL (*wearily*) Oh, Lord! (*Then firmly*) We stopped at two. "The Valiant Soldier" in the Edgware Road—

BARBARA (*taking crockery from the dresser to the tray*) H'm', *Five* minutes after you'd started!

BASIL. Well—George had to see a man . . .

BARBARA (*muttering*) I'll bet he had! I'm sorry for the *man!*

BASIL. Then we called in at some place at Horley. You see, Delia . . .

BARBARA (*taking knives and forks from the dresser to the tray*) I suppose she had to see a man as well!

BASIL (*desperately*) Look, Babs! You're not going to be like *this* all the time they're staying with us, are you?

BARBARA. Every single minute! And, I imagine, for at least a week after they've gone!

BASIL. Oh, my God!

BARBARA. After that I shall divorce you for Mental Cruelty!

BASIL. *You'll* divorce *me* . . . !

BARBARA. Are you going for your bath, or aren't you?

BASIL (*moving towards the connecting door*) I'd drown myself in the damn thing if I could be sure old George wouldn't come and yank me out again. (*He goes through into the living-room and again automatically plumps the same cushion on the settee before going up the stairs*)

(BARBARA *busies herself in the kitchen. Water can be heard running, upstairs*)

BASIL (*stopping on the stairs and listening with his ear cocked; mutters*) Oh, hell!

(*A door bangs upstairs, and* GEORGE's *voice is heard*)

GEORGE (*off*) Hy'a, Bas!

BASIL (*not so heartily*) Hy'a, George!

GEORGE (*off*) You weren't wanting the bathroom, were you, old boy?

BASIL (*calling upstairs; bravely*) No, no, carry on, old man!

GEORGE (*off*) Sure, now?

BASIL. Yes, rather!

GEORGE. Quite sure?

BASIL (*almost irritably*) Quite!

(GEORGE PADSTOW *enters on the stairs*)

GEORGE (*as he runs down*) But look, old boy, if *you'd* rather have it first . . . !

(GEORGE PADSTOW *is about Basil's age—perhaps a year or two older. He, too, is in pyjamas and dressing gown—both of vivid and clashing hues. His hair is very much in need of a comb. He sports a largish moustache. What George lacks in intelligence is made up for in "bonhomie"*)

BASIL (*coming back into the room, to the fireplace*) No, no. Honestly. It's quite all right, George.

GEORGE (*coming well into the room*) I believe you're only saying that to . . .

BASIL. Good heavens, no! It doesn't matter at all, honestly.

GEORGE (*moving above the sofa*) But, look, old man, I don't want to interfere with your usual routine while we're down here.

BASIL. But you're *not*—

GEORGE. And I'm sure Delia doesn't either.

BASIL (*wearying of this a little*) No, no. (*He sits in the armchair*) That's all right, old boy.

GEORGE. I mean if you usually have your bath at this time, I don't mind waiting, honestly I don't. (*He sits on the settee*)

BASIL (*rising; with an attempt at firmness*) Look, George, old boy, it doesn't matter a damn to me when I have it—I mean it isn't as if I had to rush out to an office or anything is it?

GEORGE. No—no. That is so, of course.

BASIL. Then, that's settled. (*He sits again*)

GEORGE. But all the same . . . Well, it *is* your house and your bathroom, isn't it?

BASIL. Yes, but . . .

GEORGE. And an Englishman's home is his castle, isn't it?

BASIL (*almost bleating*) George . . . !

GEORGE. And Delia and I—well, we have rather forced ourselves on you, haven't we? I say, have you got a cigarette, old man?

BASIL (*rising to the fireplace*) Yes, of course! (*Getting a cigarette-box, opening it and holding it out without looking in it*)

GEORGE (*rising to R of Basil*) Good old Bas! (*He puts his hand into the box, then looks in it*) Oh!

BASIL. What's the matter?

GEORGE. I—I can't take your last, old man! (*He moves above the coffee-table*)

BASIL (*blinking into the box*) *What?* But I—I thought I filled it when we came in last night. Good God! (*Then hastily*) I mean . . . (*Holding out the box again*) Come on, George, have it.

GEORGE (*firmly*) Not your last! Wouldn't dream of it.

BASIL (*moving L of George*) Nonsense! Go on, Take it! (*Pushing the box at him*).

GEORGE (*pushing the box away*) Certainly *not*! I'll get some . . . later.

BASIL. Now, look! This is ridiculous. (*He puts the box on the coffee-table*) I'm not in the least fussy. I'd just as soon have my pipe. (*Moving to the mantelpiece*) Where is the damn thing? (*He goes to the desk up L*)

GEORGE (*picking up the cigarette-box and following him around*) No, no! It's very noble of you, Bas, old boy, but you can't smoke your pipe before breakfast. Look! You have that—*last* cigarette, and I'll skidaddle upstairs and have my bath.

BASIL (*moving to the shelves up L C*) But . . .

GEORGE (*very quickly*) No, of course not! (*Following Basil*) It's *your* bath, isn't it?

BASIL. No, you . . .

GEORGE. Look, you have that last cigarette, then go and have *your* bath and—(*he moves round* L *of the settee*)—I'll just sit here and—and wait . . . (*He sits on the settee and puts the box on the coffee-table*)

(BASIL *moves to the fireplace.* DELIA's *voice is heard from upstairs.* DELIA's *voice is gay and not exactly "Roedean"*)

DELIA (*off*) Hy—A! !

(BARBARA, *in the kitchen, looks up puzzled*)

GEORGE (*rising*) There's Delia! (*Going to the archway and calling*) We're down here, old girl!

(DELIA *enters down the stairs*)

DELIA (*as she runs down; happily*) Wudgy, wudgy, *wee!* (*She runs into George's arms*) Pet lamb!

(DELIA BROWN *is a blonde; slightly cockney in speech; age around twenty-four. She can simper and she can spit. She wears a colourful and startling negligee*)

GEORGE (*as they go into a big hug*) Mmmmmmmmm!

(BARBARA *comes through the kitchen door just as Delia and George go into their clinch. She glares at them, then at Basil.* BASIL *winces.* BARBARA *returns to the kitchen.* GEORGE *and* DELIA *do not notice this*)

(*At last, breaking away slightly*) I say, poppet, you haven't got a cigarette, have you?

(BASIL *picks up the box*)

DELIA (*pouting*) Mmmm . . . no! I was just going to ask *you* . . . !
BASIL (*rushing up to Delia with the box*) Look! There's one here!
DELIA. Oh, lovely! (*She snatches the cigarette from the box*).
GEORGE (*quickly taking it from her*) No, I'm sorry, duckie! You can't have that one. It's poor old Bas's last!
BASIL (*moving* L *of the sofa*) But, George, I've told you—it doesn't matter a bit. I—I—(*automatically*)—I'd just as soon have my pipe. (*Very irritably*) Where is the damn thing. (*He moves below the sofa to* R)

(GEORGE *follows him absently.* DELIA *follows George, who still has the cigarette, purposefully*)

DELIA (*muttering to George*) But, George. I'm just dying for a cigarette.
GEORGE (*putting the cigarette back in the box*) Sorry and all that, ducks, but we can't deprive old Bas of . . . (*Suddenly*) What are you looking for, old man?

(DELIA *moves to the fireplace*)

BASIL (*still holding the box*) My blasted pipe! I had it last night.
GEORGE. Come on! Have a scout round. See if you can find old

Bas's pipe. (*He begins searching, throwing the settee cushions, papers, etc., around as he does so*)

BASIL (*tidying up* R *of the sofa*) No—please—don't bother.

GEORGE. No trouble at all, is it Delia? (*He moves* L *to Delia*)

DELIA. What's it look like?

GEORGE (*looking at her negligée*) Smashing!

DELIA (*kissing him*) Silly! I meant the pipe!

GEORGE. Oh, the . . . ! (*He crosses Delia to the mantelpiece*) What's it look like, Bas, old man?

BASIL. What does what . . . ? (*He is still searching, on his knees,* R *of the sofa*)

GEORGE. The pipe?

BASIL (*almost irritably*) Well, it's just—just . . . (*He makes vague movements with his hands*)

GEORGE (*happily*) Oh, yes. (*Looking on the mantelpiece*) I know the kind.

(*They are all searching.* DELIA *moves above the settee and looks over the back of it.*

BARBARA *suddenly looks up alarmed*)

BARBARA. What on earth . . . ? (*She listens for a fraction of a second, then rushes to the back door and opens it*)

(*A jet of water is spurting down onto the doorstep from above*)

Oh my . . . ! (*She shuts the door and rushes quickly through into the living-room, almost falling over Delia in her frantic rush towards the hall*)

DELIA (*as she is pushed aside by Barbara*) Ow! (*Then seeing who it is*) Oh, good morning, Barbara. We're just looking for . . .

GEORGE (*brightly*) 'Morning, Barbara!

(*But* BARBARA *has torn up the stairs and out of sight*)

I say, what . . . ?

BASIL (*alarmed; rushing to the archway*) You all right, Babs?

(*The only reply is a door slam from upstairs.* BASIL *comes back into the room.* DELIA *moves* L, *to* R *of George*)

GEORGE. Is she?

BASIL. Is she what?

GEORGE. All right?

BASIL. I—I think she's—just—er . . .

GEORGE (*hastily*) Oh, yes, of course! I see. How stupid of me!

(BASIL *blinks at him*)

DELIA. Do you think it would be all right if I had the first bath?

BASIL. I—I . . .

DELIA. I'm no use at all until I've had my bath.

GEORGE (*smirking*) Oh! I wouldn't say *that!* (*He smacks her bottom lightly*).

DELIA (*giggling*) Oh! Isn't he awful? Basil, don't you think he's awful?

BASIL (*looking on the shelves up* C; *still distrait*) Who?

DELIA. George Padstow?

BASIL. Who? George . . . ? Oh! (*Pulling himself together*) Old George! Yes, awful!

GEORGE (*noticing Basil's lack of concentration*) I say, there's nothing wrong, is there, old man?

BASIL. No. no. Why? What should be wrong?

GEORGE. You don't seem to be *with* us—quite.

BASIL (*moving towards the kitchen door*) Well—it's just that—Barbara—that is—*we* didn't think *you'd* be with *us*—not *quite* so early, I mean. We haven't got the place squared up, as you can see, and—well I'm afraid—(*opening kitchen door and peeping through*)—breakfast won't be ready for a while yet. *Quite* a while, by the look of things.

GEORGE. My dear old boy, there's no need to apologize . . .

BASIL. I wasn't apologizing exactly. I—(*muttering*)—I was just stating a fact.

DELIA (*moving slowly above the settee*) Oh, but I shan't be ready for ages, so there's no need to rush. It takes me hours to put a face on.

GEORGE. A face on what?

DELIA. My face, of course, silly! But if I could have the first bath . . .

(BARBARA *enters and comes downstairs to above the settee. She is carrying the tray with the empty tea-cups on it*)

BASIL (*nervously*) Hel . . . hello, Barbara. Er . . . how are things going?

(*She glares at a cushion on the floor* R *of the settee.*)

BARBARA. The bath water's gone! (*With painful calm, moving up* L *of the settee*) Good morning—George! Good morning—Delia!

(GEORGE *and* DELIA *murmur* "*Good mornings*" *in reply*)

BASIL (*picking up the cushion* R *of the settee*) How do you mean—gone? Gone where?

BARBARA. Through the overflow, thank God! (*Moving down* L *of the settee*) Someone must have left the hot tap running.

GEORGE. Oh, my Lord! I say, I'm frightfully . . .

BARBARA (*smiling with an effort*) I don't mind—if you don't mind—mind a cold bath, I mean.

GEORGE (*hesitantly*) No—I—I don't mind. Er—Delia, do you mind?

DELIA. Does it take long to hot up again?

BARBARA. Hours!

BASIL (*trying to laugh*) Well, *one* hour, shall we say?

BARBARA (*quietly*) No, don't let's say that. (*She moves below the settee*) Let's say what I said originally—hours. (*Smiling frigidly at Basil*) You *know* the heater isn't working properly.

BASIL. Oh, no. Of course it isn't—is it?

BARBARA. NO!

BASIL. NO!

(*There is a moment of awkward silence*)

BASIL (*with a shrug*) Oh, well . . . !

BARBARA (*holding the tray under Basil's nose*) Basil, would you mind—extracting the soggy cigarette end from that cup?

(BASIL *drops the cushion, blinks into one of the cups and pulls a face*)

(*Continuing, but speaking generally*) Silly of me, but I've always had a horror of extracting soggy cigarette ends from cups.

(BASIL *performs the operation and stands with the cigarette end between finger and thumb*)

Thank you, Basil. You were always—so brave!

(BASIL *does not know what to do with cigarette end. Almost automatically he opens cigarette-box, which is still in his hand, and is about to drop end in it*)

(*Very "sweetly"*) Not in there, *darling*! Surely . . .

(GEORGE *rushes across to* L *of Basil with an ashtray from the mantelpiece which is filled to overflowing.* BASIL *stubs the cigarette end on to the pile rather heavily, with the result that several cigarette ends fall to the floor.* BASIL *looks at them, then puts the box on the mantelpiece.* BARBARA *looks at them and so does* GEORGE. GEORGE *then moves* R *of the settee to above it*)

(*At last; quietly, but meaningly*) The brush and pan are in the kitchen.

(BARBARA *goes to connecting door, tray in hand, and opens it.* GEORGE *moves* L *and replaces the ashtray on the mantelpiece. He and Delia are rather subdued.* BASIL *rushes up to Barbara*)

BASIL (*under his breath*) Let me—I'll take that. (*He grabs the tray from her, speaking sotto voce*) You stay and talk to George and Delia.

BARBARA (*sotto voce*) What about?

BASIL (*sotto voce*) Well—ask them how they are.

(BASIL *shoots through kitchen door, almost flings the tray on the kitchen table and collapses onto the stool by it—one arm on table and head in hand*)

BARBARA (*moving* R *of the settee; in a controlled voice*) Well, George and Delia, how are you?

GEORGE (*moving* L *of the settee*) Oh, we're fine thanks. Slept like tops. Didn't we, Delia?

BARBARA (*rather sharply*) I beg your pardon.

GEORGE. I mean I slept like *a* top and I expect Delia slept like another. Eh—didn't you, Delia?

DELIA. Yes. I slept like—like a top!

GEORGE (*to Barbara. He is rather nervous of her*) Did you sleep like a . . . ? Did you sleep well?

BARBARA (*tidying the settee*) Not very, thanks. I had a headache.

GEORGE. I'm sorry. I—I hope it's gone now?

BARBARA. No, it's still around.

DELIA. You know what you should take for headaches?

BARBARA. I think mine is—taking up residence.

GEORGE. Oh, but you should take *something*, you know. What's this remedy of yours, Delia?

DELIA. Oh, it's marvellous! Aspirin.

BARBARA (*smiling, thinly*) Too dangerous! (*She puts some papers on the shelves* R)

DELIA. Not if you don't take too many.

BARBARA. I should require two doses of at least fifty each to get rid of *my* headache. (*Then quickly*) Now—what are you going to do, both of you, until breakfast time?

GEORGE. Well—er . . .

DELIA. Yes, you do that, George, and I'll help Barbara. (*She moves below the settee; to Barbara*) I'm afraid I'm not very good, but . . .

BARBARA (*smiling*) You mean—*you're not very good*—at housework and cooking?

(BARBARA *automatically begins picking up cigarette ends from floor.* DELIA *does likewise below the sofa, and* GEORGE LC)

DELIA. Yes, that's what I meant.

BARBARA. Of course! I'd hate to get any wrong ideas. (*Then quickly*) It's very sweet of you, Delia, to offer to help, but I can manage. (*Referring to Delia's solitary cigarette end*) Shall I take that?

DELIA (*emptying her cigarette end into Barbara's hands and moving* L *of George*) Cigarettes, cigarettes everywhere, and not a one to smoke!

GEORGE (*to Delia, as he crosses her to empty his own collection into Barbara's hands*) Clever girl!

DELIA (*almost blushing*) Oh, George!

(GEORGE *rubs his hands*)

BARBARA. I *must* go and see about *your* breakfasts. Er—make yourselves at home, won't you?

GEORGE. Now don't you worry about us, Barbara. Just carry on as if we weren't here.

BARBARA (*as she moves to kitchen door; muttering*) But you are, aren't you?

(GEORGE *and* DELIA *look at each other.* BARBARA *goes into the kitchen, leaving the door half open.* BASIL *leaps up guiltily*)

BASIL. I was just . . . (*He rushes to the cupboard below the sink and gets a hand brush*)

BARBARA It's done! (*Holding out her clenched hand*) Get rid of them!

(GEORGE *and* DELIA *start and look at each other again*)

BASIL (*alarmed*) What? I can't Barbara. How can I?

BARBARA (*coldly*) The cigarette ends!

BASIL. Oh!

(GEORGE *and* DELIA *show their relief.* BARBARA *puts the cigarette ends into Basil's hands*)

DELIA. Do you know, George, I thought for a moment she meant
. . . .

GEORGE (*hoarsely*) Sssh! Don't put ideas into her head!

BASIL. Where shall I put them?

BARBARA. In the dustbin—outside.

(GEORGE *and* DELIA, *almost unconsciously, move near the connecting door, eavesdropping, although they have their backs to the door*)

BASIL (*moving to the back door*) Yes, darling.

BARBARA. And you can empty this at the same time. (*She moves to the "pedal" ash-can, extracts can and hands it to Basil*)

BASIL (*taking it*) Yes, darling.

BARBARA. And while you're out there, you might look around for the cat.

BASIL. Yes, darling.

BARBARA. And when you come back I want to . . .

BASIL. You want to talk to me—*again*. Yes, darling!

(BASIL *exits* R. BARBARA, *immediately after Basil's exit, looks around desperately, also almost unconsciously, moves to the connecting door and slams it.* GEORGE *and* DELIA *give yelps of alarm as door closes.* GEORGE *sits on the settee,* DELIA *in the armchair, both rigid.* BARBARA *unobtrusively washes her hands and continues preparing breakfast things.* GEORGE *looks embarrassedly towards Delia.* DELIA *looks likewise towards George.* GEORGE *begins to hum "Rustle of Spring" very heavily. Reaching a high note he cracks on it and tails off into silence.* DELIA *steals over to him, sits on his knee and kisses his brow*)

DELIA (*almost baby fashion*) George . . .

GEORGE. Yes, old girl.

DELIA. George—I know it's silly of me. Mother tells me I have too much imagination, but I've always been very sensitive. I sense things other people don't. And—I've got a feeling right now that—that . . .

GEORGE. That what?

DELIA. We're not very welcome here.

GEORGE. Well, I've got the hide of a weatherbeaten rhinoceros and that *had* occurred to me!

DELIA. Do you think we ought to stay where we're not welcome?
GEORGE (*firmly*) Yes!
DELIA. But . . .
GEORGE. You see, duckie, it's a question of—finance.
   DELIA (*rotating and admiring her negligée*) Oh! It's silly of me, but I just don't understand finance, George. It's too complicated.
   GEORGE. There's nothing complicated about something that doesn't exist! What it boils down to is, that if we don't stay here, we don't stay anywhere, because we can't afford to. See?
   DELIA. Uh-huh! (*After a slight pause she rises and moves* L) After all—putting us up for a fortnight—well, that's the least they can do, isn't it, considering you once saved Basil's life.
   GEORGE (*grandly*) Oh, that was nothing!
   DELIA. I wonder if Barbara knows that: that you rescued Basil from drowning.
   GEORGE. I expect Basil's mentioned it.
   DELIA (*sitting on his knee again*) If he has then shouldn't Barbara be grateful?
   GEORGE. From what I've seen this morning, I should say she'll never forgive me!
   DELIA (*flinging herself across his knees*) Well, you'll never be able to say that I wasn't grateful, will you, George?
   GEORGE. Er—no, old girl. (*With a glance towards the kitchen door*) Do you think we ought—(*He is referring to their positions on the settee*)— I don't know that Barbara would approve . . .
   DELIA (*sweeping on*) When you rescued me from the river at Richmond, I showed my gratitude, didn't I?

   (BARBARA *starts loading the tray*)

   GEORGE (*with a smirk*) I'm sure you did, but you were showing so much else at the time . . .
   DELIA (*squeaking with mock horror*) George Padstow! (*She slaps him playfully*) Aren't you awful!
   GEORGE (*smirking*) Am I?
   DELIA. Angel! (*She kisses him fervently*) Wouldn't it have been awful, George, if I hadn't fallen in the river that day?
   GEORGE. Would it?
   DELIA. We should never have met.
   GEORGE. H'm! What is it old Shakespeare says? "There is a— whatnot that shapes our something or other." He certainly knew what he was talking about!
   DELIA (*with a whimper*) Oh, George! Just three weeks ago today!
   GEORGE. How time flies! (*He pulls Delia to him and they snuggle up together*)

   (BARBARA *comes through the kitchen door. She knocks the tray against the door with a crash as she comes through.* GEORGE *and* DELIA *leap apart.* DELIA *rises very quickly, and straightens her negligee, moving to the fireplace.*)

DELIA (*nervously*) Hello—Barbara! Er—can I do anything?
BARBARA. No, thank you. Just carry on—er—carrying on! (*She takes the tray to the table up* C, *opens the leaves, and starts to lay it*)
DELIA (*moving* L *of Barbara; nervously*) I—I—I was just saying to George how funny it was.
BARBARA. What was?
DELIA. That he should have saved Basil from drowning.
BARBARA (*after a quick look at her*) My sense of humour was never my strong point.
DELIA (*quickly*) Oh, I don't mean it was funny *that* way.
BARBARA. *No?*
DELIA (*laying a knife and fork in a desultory fashion*) No. I mean it's funny because he saved *me* from drowning too—three weeks ago!
BARBARA (*intent on the table*) Fancy now!
DELIA (*coyly*) That's how we met—isn't it, George?
GEORGE. 'S'right!
BARBARA. Well, well! (*After a look at Delia's laying*) Is George left-handed?
DELIA. I don't think so. (*Moving* L *of the settee*) You're not left-handed, are you, George?
GEORGE (*heartily*) Rather not. Nothing peculiar about me.
BARBARA. In that case . . . (*She changes position of knife and fork*) How lucky for you, Delia, that Basil wasn't a girl.
DELIA (*puzzled*) Basil wasn't a girl! When? (*She moves to the fire-place*)
BARBARA. When George saved him from drowning.
DELIA (*more puzzled*) But—er—is he *now?*
BARBARA (*moving above* L *of the settee; heavily*) The point I'm trying to make is—George saved you from drowning and promptly got engaged to you. He saved Basil first. Well . . . !
GEORGE. But good Lord, I was only fifteen at the time!
BARBARA (*with a look at him*) A very enterprising fifteen, I'll be bound! (*She returns to the table*)

(DELIA *after a look at Barbara, and not knowing quite what is expected of her, gives a noisy and somewhat false giggle.* BASIL, *ash-can in hand, enters kitchen from outside just as Delia giggles. Hearing her, he rushes through the connecting door*)

BASIL (*as he charges in; in great alarm*) What's up?

(DELIA *immediately stops giggling. There is a silence while all the others look at Basil blankly*)

What . . . ?
BARBARA (*coldly*) And *what* is the matter with you?
BASIL. Someone's in anguish—I heard them!
BARBARA (*with meaning*) I never made a sound.
GEORGE (*cheerfully*) It was Delia you heard, old boy, laughing.
BASIL (*blinking*) Oh! Is that what it was?

BARBARA (*quietly*) *That's* what it was.

BASIL. Oh! I see! (*After an "unseeing" look at Delia; to Barbara*) Well, how are things going?

BARBARA (*snatching the ash-can from him and speaking with ironic heartiness as she crosses to the kitchen door*) Never say die!

(BARBARA *goes into the kitchen. There is a silence for a moment, then, suddenly* BASIL, DELIA *and* GEORGE *all move simultaneously towards the stairs*)

BASIL		I'll just go and wash!
GEORGE	(*together*)	I'll just go and wash!
DELIA		I must go and wash!

(*They all stop dead, look at each other, then grin feebly*)

BASIL		(*feebly to Delia*) Look, you go!
GEORGE	(*together*)	(*to Basil*) Carry on, Bas!
DELIA		(*to George*) George, you go.

BASIL. Oh, hell! (*He crosses to the fireplace*)

GEORGE (*following him to* LC) Now look, old man, we've got to come to an understanding about this sort of thing. And Delia and I are very determined, aren't we, Delia?

DELIA (*moving above the settee*) Yes. What about?

(BASIL *picks up the cigarette-box*)

GEORGE. While we're here we cannot—we must not, in any way, interfere with your routine—yours and Barbara's!

DELIA (*blankly*) We haven't got one.

GEORGE (*testily*) I'm talking to Basil!

DELIA. Oh! (*As she moves towards the stairs*) Well, while you're talking I'll . . .

(DELIA *exits upstairs*)

GEORGE (*almost overlapping, to Basil*) As I've said before, old man, this is *your* home—your castle—your—your . . .

BASIL (*sitting in the armchair; wearily*) Just let's say it's mine—that is, the Building Society's and mine.

GEORGE (*rather irritably*) Well, it will be all yours one day, so . . .

BASIL. Not if they can help it!

GEORGE (*more irritably*) *Who* can help it?

BASIL. The blasted Building Society!

GEORGE (*pulling Basil up and passing him across to* R *of himself*) Look, old man, we're not discussing Building Societies.

BASIL. Aren't we?

GEORGE. No! I am pointing out that you have the moral right to the first wash! Delia and I . . . (*He looks around*) Where the devil is she?

BASIL (*looking upstairs and listening*) Up there!

GEORGE. What's she . . . ?

BASIL. She's washing!

GEORGE. No! Look! (*Crossing Basil to the stairs*) I'll go and fetch her down by the hair of her head.

BASIL (*moving above the coffee-table*) Leave here where she is. Er—George . . .

GEORGE. Yes, old man?

(BARBARA *exits* R *with kitchen rubbish*)

BASIL. After breakfast I hope you won't mind if . . .

(DELIA'S *voice is heard from upstairs*)

DELIA (*off*) Hy-ya!

GEORGE (*moving to the stairs and calling*) Hy-ya!

(BASIL *winces, moves below the settee and sits* L)

DELIA (*off*) Geo-orge!

GEORGE. Finished washing?

DELIA (*off*) Don't be silly, poppet, I haven't started.

GEORGE. Well, hurry up. Basil wants . . .

DELIA (*off*) Will you ask Basil for some soap?

GEORGE. Soap!

DELIA (*off*) There doesn't seem to be any in the bathroom.

GEORGE (*coming into the room*) There doesn't seem to be any soap in the bathroom, old boy.

BASIL (*with a nervous look towards the kitchen*) Er . . . soap.

(BARBARA *enters the kitchen from* R)

GEORGE. Soap.

BASIL (*rising and moving* L *and above the settee*) I—I'll get some. (*Unconsciously handing the cigarette-box to George*) Cigarette?

GEORGE (*taking the cigarette out of the box*) Thanks.

(BASIL *moves on below George to the kitchen.* GEORGE *sits* R *on the settee and lights the cigarette*)

BARBARA (*with some irritation*) Now what is it?

BASIL (*jumping*) Er—nothing—I . . . (*He moves to the dresser*)

BARBARA. Then go away. Get back to your friends.

BASIL. I—I—just wanted . . .

BARBARA (*hardly listening*) Wanted what? (*She takes the bacon back to the fridge*)

BASIL. Er—nothing—I—Don't let me interrupt you. You just—er—carry on. (*He whistles nervously as he goes on searching for the soap. He moves things and occasionally takes something out and fails to put it back*)

BARBARA (*when she finally sees what he is doing*) What are you looking for?

BASIL (*with attempted airiness*) It's all right. I can manage. You just—er—carry on!

BARBARA. Damn it! (*Turning back to the fridge*) Aren't I carrying on?

BASIL. I—er . . . (*Suddenly finding what he wants*) Aaah! (*He produces a half-pound carton of household carbolic soap*)
BARBARA (*still with her back to him*) What are you "Aaah-ing" about?
BASIL. Nothing. Er—carry on! (*He darts quickly into the living-room*)

(*As the door closes,* BARBARA *turns round and gapes at it. Then seeing things Basil has left lying about, she gives a wail of anguish and begins putting them back*)

BASIL (*moving above the settee*) Here we are, George. Give this to Delia, will you? (*He gives George the soap and moves* L)
GEORGE (*no reaction from him at the size or kind of soap, as he takes the carton*) Yes, rather. Thanks old man. (*He rises to the stairs and calls*) Yoo-hoo!
DELIA (*off*) Yoo-hoo!

(BASIL *winces and sits gloomily* L *on the settee*)

(*Off*) Is that you, George. Have you . . . ?
GEORGE. Yes, catch! (*He throws the carton upstairs*)

(DELIA *gives a little scream as carton nears her*)

Well caught, Bedser!
DELIA (*off—she has obviously seen name on carton—in dismay*) Oh! But George . . . !
GEORGE. What's up, old girl?
DELIA (*off, in dismay*) Oh—er—nothing.
GEORGE (*heartily*) Good! Yell out when you're through with the bathroom. (*He comes back into the room*) Now . . . what were you saying, Bas, old boy?

(*There is a strident ring at the front door bell.* BARBARA *comes in from the kitchen*)

BARBARA. That'll be the post.
BASIL. I'll go.

(BASIL *rises and goes off into the hall, unconsciously taking a cushion with him*)

BARBARA. You're not washed, George.
GEORGE. No.
BARBARA. I wonder why.
GEORGE (*moving to the fireplace*) Oh. Well, Delia's in the bathroom at the moment. I'd better wait until she comes out, don't you think?
BARBARA. I do.

(BASIL *returns with one letter—and the cushion*)

BARBARA. Anything for me?
BASIL. No, only one for me. (*Looking at the envelope*) It's from Herbert. (*Moving to George*) My agent, Herbert Henkins.

(BARBARA *picks up the tray from the table up* C)

GEORGE (*patting Basil on the back*) Good man!

BASIL. Who? Herbert Henkins?

GEORGE. No. You! It must be wonderful having letters rolling up from your agent with big fat royalty cheques in them.

BARBARA (*moving towards the kitchen door*) It must indeed! (*Turning at the door*) D'you think Delia is going to be long?

GEORGE. Er—(*with a smirk*)—well, you know what women are.

BARBARA. I do. I didn't until I married. But I do now! (*She goes through into the kitchen*)

BASIL (*uneasily, to George*) You must excuse Barbara. She isn't—er—at her best early in the morning. (*He sits* L *on the settee and opens his letter*) Excuse me.

GEORGE. You? You mean you aren't at your best either? (*Seeing Basil reading the letter*) Oh, I get you!

BASIL (*having read the letter*) Oh, hell! Hell and damnation! Sorry, George!

(*During the following,* BARBARA *puts the sausages and bacon on a dish on the oven top, takes a clean towel from the cupboard and puts it by the sink, then puts bread, sauce bottle and condiments on the tray*)

GEORGE. Bad news?

BASIL. My play . . .

GEORGE. Your what?

BASIL. My play. I wrote it.

GEORGE (*with awe*) Go on! (*Moving* L *of the settee*) I say! Ruddy Shakespeare, eh? I thought you only wrote novels. I didn't know you wrote plays as well.

BASIL. I've only written one.

GEORGE. When's it going on?

BASIL. As far as I can gather, never! Four managers have turned it down already.

GEORGE (*in great disgust*) Twerps!

BASIL. And this is to tell me that a fifth has done the same.

GEORGE (*grunting*) Like a lot of sheep those fellows: (*Moving to the fireplace*) No individuality.

BASIL (*brightening as he reads further*) Ah!

GEORGE (*also brightening*) Good news?

BASIL. Henkins says not to give up hope. He says Faith Brantingham is trying to find another play, so he's sent her mine to read.

GEORGE (*with awe and admiration*) I say!

BASIL. *What* do you say?

GEORGE. Faith Brantingham, eh?

BASIL. Yes. Why do you . . . ?

GEORGE (*thoughtfully*) Forty-one—nineteen—thirty-six.

BASIL. I beg your pardon?

GEORGE. Faith Brantingham. (*With gestures*) Vital statistics. I read 'em in the paper last week. So did Delia; sulked for the rest of the day. You see, Delia's thirty—twenty-six—thirty-eight. Not so good, is it?

BASIL. Are you asking me?

GEORGE. Well—er—yes.

BASIL. I wish you wouldn't! (*Rising to* R *of the settee and above it*) Faith Brantingham! Wouldn't say she's *ideal* for the part exactly, but—if she'd *do* the play—it would be marvellous! (*He moves* L *of the settee*)

GEORGE. I'll say it would! You'd pack 'em in! I mean to say . . ! Forty-one—nineteen—thirty-six!

BASIL (*moving* R *of George*) George, as her part in my play would be that of an excessively devout nun I don't see that "forty-one—nineteen—thirty-six" enters into it.

GEORGE. But they'll put in a scene where she strips down to the essentials, won't they?

BASIL. They will—over my battered and bleeding body!!

GEORGE (*indignantly*) But, Bas, old boy—God forbid that I should try to teach you your job, but you *must* give the public what they *want*—and as far as Faith Brantingham is concerned, what they want is . . .

BASIL. "Forty-one—nineteen—thirty-six".

GEORGE. Precisely!

BASIL. H'm! (*Moving to the french windows*) Anyway, she isn't playing it yet. (*Dolefully*) She may not even bother to read it. (*With a start*) Good Lord!

GEORGE. What's up?

BASIL. I've just remembered! (*Moving to the table up* C) She's at the Theatre Royal here this week! The show she's in at the moment closed in London on Saturday and they're touring for a few weeks before finishing altogether.

GEORGE. Then why don't you go down to the theatre and see her—tell her how marvellous your play is?

BASIL. She might not believe me.

(BARBARA *comes from the kitchen with her tray*)

(*Seeing her; nervously*) Oh—er—hello!

GEORGE (*equally so*) Er—hello! (*Moving* L *of Basil*) Better?

BARBARA (*sharply*) I beg your pardon?

GEORGE (*hurriedly*) I meant—er—hello!

BARBARA (*with a somewhat freezing look*) Hy-a! Delia not down yet?

GEORGE. Not yet.

BASIL (*limply*) She's washing.

BARBARA. H'm! Well, your breakfast's ready. If it stays on the stove too long it'll be spoilt.

GEORGE (*alarmed*) Oh, no!

BARBARA. Oh, yes! And you two aren't washed yet. You'd better go through into the kitchen. You don't mind washing in the kitchen, George?

GEORGE (*heartily*) Me? (*Crossing to* R *of Basil*) Good Lord, no!
I love it!

BARBARA. Do you now? Well, off you go and enjoy yourself.
You too, Basil, I've put a clean towel out. (*She moves towards table with
tray*)

(GEORGE *is in her way.*)

Excuse me!

(*They dodge once or twice then* GEORGE *and* BASIL *go through into
kitchen.* BARBARA *moves to table, and transfers the things from the tray*)

GEORGE (*as he looks around kitchen*) I say!
BASIL. What! (*He crosses George to down* R)
GEORGE. I like this!
BASIL. The kitchen?
GEORGE. Yes. Kind of dinky, isn't it?
BASIL. I wish you'd mention it to Barbara. She's very house-
proud. It might—er—brighten her up a bit.
GEORGE. Oh! Then I will! (*He moves to the connecting door*)
BASIL. Just mention it—er—casually sometime.
GEORGE. Barbara!
BARBARA (*at table*) Yes?
GEORGE. The kitchen.
BARBARA. What about it?
GEORGE. I think it's dinky.
BARBARA. Do you?
GEORGE. Yes, rather!
BARBARA (*almost smiling*) Thank you, George.
GEORGE. Basil asked me to tell you. Said it might brighten you
up a bit.

(BASIL *hearing this, freezes in his tracks.* BARBARA *opens her mouth
to speak furiously, but as* GEORGE's *head has disappeared, she says
nothing*)

(*Joining Basil*) I told her.

(BASIL, *speechless, indicates the sink, and runs some water in the bowl—
or indicates for* GEORGE *to go behind screen*)

BASIL (*in hollow voice*) George . . .

(GEORGE *begins to wash—or disappear behind screen*)

BARBARA (*at the table, suddenly, to herself*) Oh! (*She hurries to
connecting door and goes through into the kitchen; addressing the men*) Just a
minute! You can't . . . Let
me get you some soap. (*She goes to the dresser*)
GEORGE. Eh?
BASIL. There *is* soap here already.

BARBARA (*going to the cupboard*) For heaven's sake! He can't use that. That's for scrubbing floors and sinks and . . . (*Finding and unwrapping a tablet of toilet soap*) You don't want the man to pull all the skin off his face, do you? Here, George, use this. (*She hands him the soap*)

GEORGE (*sniffing the soap; appreciatively*) H'mm! Lemon!

BARBARA (*shortly*) Lavender.

GEORGE. Oh! (*He continues washing*)

BARBARA. Now do hurry up, both of you. I'm taking the breakfast through. (*She takes the coffee, milk, and dish of bacon and sausages through into the living-room and sets them out on the table*)

BASIL (*meanwhile; apprehensively*) George, do you mind if I wash at the same time as you? Barbara . . .

GEORGE. Of course not, old man. Muck in.

(BASIL *and* GEORGE *wash together.*

DELIA, *with a very red face, now comes downstairs and into the living-room and moves down* LC)

DELIA (*plaintively*) George . . . (*Seeing he isn't there*) Oh!

BARBARA (*without turning*) Oh, there you are, Delia!

DELIA (*wretchedly*) Yes, here I am.

BARBARA (*hearing the misery in her voice, turns*) Breakfast is . . . (*Looking at her face*) Delia! Your face! (*She moves above the settee*)

DELIA. I know! It's awful, isn't it?

BARBARA. Hideous!

DELIA (*with a howl*) Ohhh! And it's so sore.

BARBARA. What is it? A rash? (*Coming* R *of Delia*) Good heavens! *Not* scarlet fever?

DELIA (*yelling*) No, no!

BARBARA (*unheeding*) That's what it looks like to me! (*Heavily*) Scarlet fever! Quarantine! All shut up together for weeks on end . . .! *Is* there a God?

DELIA (*tearfully*) But it isn't! It's . . .

(GEORGE *finishes washing and starts towards the door*)

BARBARA. Well, whatever it is something's got to be done about it! I suppose we'd better get the doctor to check up on you right away—before you have your breakfast, and it's all ready. Oh, my Lord! (*Moving to the telephone*) What's his number? (*She rushes to the connecting door, meeting George*) Basil! (*Irritably*) Out of my way, George! (*She pushes past George and calls through into the kitchen*) Basil! What's the doctor's telephone number, do you know?

BASIL (*in alarm, as he comes through into the living-room, towel in hand*) Doctor? Why—what . . . ?

BARBARA. Delia's got scarlet fever or rabies or something!

BASIL } (*together*) { What?
GEORGE }

BARBARA. Well, *look* at her.

(GEORGE *goes to* L *of Delia.* BASIL *to* R *of her. They peer into her face.*
DELIA *whimpers*)

BASIL. Horrible! Is it scarlet fever?
GEORGE. Looks more like drink to me! (*Accusingly, to Delia*)
Have you been at that bottle of gin in my case?

(DELIA *gives George a hearty smack on the face*)

(*Recoiling from the blow*) I say! Steady as she goes, old girl. I only
asked!
DELIA. George Padstow, I'll never speak to you again.
BASIL. Once the doctor's seen you I doubt if you'll have the
chance for months!
DELIA. Oh! ! ! (*Almost in tears*) Oh, Basil! (*She unconsciously leans
on him*)
BASIL (*as his arm goes round her unconsciously*) There, there, poor
Delia!
BARBARA (*after an enormous clearing of the throat, moving* R *of Basil*)
If you don't mind scarlet fever, Basil, you might at least mind
George and me!
DELIA (*shouting*) Can't you get it into your heads, all of you, that
it isn't scarlet fever?
GEORGE (*muttering*) Or drink?
DELIA (*fuming*) Ooooh!

(DELIA *turns and dashes out into the hall and up the stairs*)

BASIL (*quickly*) Barbara! Oughtn't you to dash after her?
BARBARA (*crossing George to down* L*; coldly*) I am *not* a greyhound!
GEORGE (*unperturbed; moving up* C *and looking at the table*) I say!
This looks top-hole! Bacon and sausage, and lots of "Dip"!
BASIL (*moving up* R *of the settee; horrified*) George! Can you think
about bacon and sausages and "Dip" when poor dear darling
Delia . . .
BARBARA (*acidly*) I beg your pardon?
BASIL (*snapping*) I'm talking about *his* poor dear darling Delia.
BARBARA (*with meaning*) I know you are! George, aren't you
worried?
GEORGE (*looking at the dish*) I'll say I am! The dip's beginning to
congeal.

(DELIA *enters from upstairs. She has one hand behind her back*)

DELIA (*almost triumphantly*) Now!
GEORGE (*sitting* L *at the table*) Thank God! Now we can start!
DELIA (*very hoity-toity*) If nobody had mentioned my face I was
going to do likewise. After all I *hope* I have *some* manners. (*She
crosses below George to* L *of him*)
BARBARA (*it is almost a mutter*) We all do—fervently!
DELIA (*moving to* R *of Barbara*) But I must say, Barbara, I'm rather

surprised that you haven't a little more consideration for your guests!

BARBARA. Delia, what are you talking about?

DELIA. I mean to say! To ask anyone—especially a girl who takes a pride in her appearance—to wash with *this*! (*From behind her back she produces the large and by now, wet and rather "suddy" half-pound bar of household carbolic soap and holds it out to Barbara*) No wonder my face is red! I wonder it's there at all!

BARBARA (*gaping at soap*) Where on earth did you get that from?

DELIA (*accusingly and quickly*) Didn't you give it to Basil to give to George to give to me?

(BASIL *goes to the kitchen with the towel*)

BARBARA. I did *not*! Do you think I have no more sense than to . . . I would never have dreamed of . . . (*Suddenly remembering*) Basil! (*Crossing below Delia to the kitchen door*) Is that what you were turning the kitchen upside down to find just now?

BASIL. I—er—I . . .

BARBARA. Why didn't you tell me you were looking for soap? (*To Delia*) Delia, I'm so sorry! (*To Basil*) Oh! I could kill you!

GEORGE. Let him have his breakfast first.

BARBARA. Carbolic!

DELIA (*with fine scorn*) Breakfast! That's all you think about, isn't it?

GEORGE. Yes.

DELIA. It doesn't matter to you that I'm in agony, does it?

GEORGE (*with his eye on the dish*) I've got a one-track mind.

DELIA (*shouting*) Well, I'm glad I've found you out, George Padstow, before it's too late!

GEORGE. But it *is*, duckie.

DELIA (*with a yelp*) What? ? ?

GEORGE. Far too late!

DELIA. What are you . . . ?

GEORGE. Have you forgotten—on the settee, at your mother's last Tuesday night?

(*There is a horrified silence for a moment*)

BARBARA (*horrified*) Well, really . . . !

BASIL (*also horrified*) George! *Please*!

DELIA (*likewise*) George Padstow!

GEORGE (*picking up a spoon*) Can I help myself, Barbara?

DELIA (*gibbering with rage*) You *dare* say a thing like that!

GEORGE. Truth will out!

DELIA (*livid*) Oooh! (*Crossing to L of Barbara*) Basil, Barbara, you don't believe him, do you?

BARBARA (*muttering*) Truth will out!

DELIA. It isn't true. (*To George*) Tell them it isn't true you rat!

GEORGE (*with eyes and interest on the dish*) But it *is*.

Delia. Oooh!

George. Last Tuesday night I asked her to marry me.

Delia (*between relief and anger*) Of *course* you did, but that isn't what you . . .

George. Admitted I was pretty well ginned up at the time, but there it is. I popped the question, and she couldn't say "yes" quick enough, could you, ducks? (*Patiently*) Last Tuesday night on the settee at your mother's, you said you'd marry me.

Delia (*furiously*) Why didn't you say that in the first place, instead of making Basil and Barbara think . . . !

George (*pensively*) I *would* like my breakfast!

Delia (*fuming*) Go on, then! Have your breakfast you evil-minded elephant you! And I hope it *poisons* you!

Barbara (*to Delia, bridling*) Are you suggesting that *my* cooking . . . ?

Basil (*coming between Barbara and Delia*) Now, Babs, please . . . !

Delia (*raging, her mind still on George*) And to make certain that it does—there! (*And on the "There" she plants the bar of soap in the middle of the dish of bacon and sausages with a splash and rubs it well and truly in*)

George (*alarmed*) I say! Steady as she . . . (*Realizing what has happened*) Blimey!

Basil (*in horror*) Delia!

Barbara (*likewise*) No! Oh . . . No!

(*There is a moment of horrified silence as they all look at the dish, then* Delia, *realizing the enormity of her offence, begins, first to whimper, then works up to a thorough howl. As she does so, she runs* L *of the settee, round below it, and off up the stairs.* George *rises, and they all follow her with their eyes. Again there is silence for a moment*)

George (*at last, in a low throbbing voice*) I'll scalp her! (*He picks up the plate*) I'll carve her into little pieces! I'll pull her finger nails out one by one!

(Barbara *stands quivering with suppressed rage*)

Basil (*plaintively, his hand to stomach*) For *God's* sake, shut up!

George (*his voice rising*) She can't do that to *me*! (*He puts the plate down and moves to the fireplace*) We're not married *yet*!

Basil (*turning apprehensively to Barbara*) Babs—darling.

Barbara (*slowly, in an only just controlled voice*) Basil—take George into the garden.

Basil. What?

Barbara. And show him the hollyhocks.

Basil (*gaping*) But—Babs . . .

Barbara (*at breaking point; giving every word full value*) Basil—will you *please* take George into the garden and show him the hollyhocks?

(Basil *gapes at her, then backs away*)

BASIL (*almost mumbling as he takes George by the arm*) Come and see the hollyhocks, old man. (*He leads him to the french windows*)

GEORGE (*as he is led to the french windows*) My favourite breakfast! Bacon—sausages—dip!

BASIL (*it is still almost a mumble*) We've got three red ones and two cream ones.

(BASIL *and* GEORGE *exit into the garden.* BARBARA *stands quite still for a moment, then moves slowly to the table and picks up the dish with both hands. She regards it tragically for a moment, and then, her pent up feelings release themselves. Like Delia, she begins softly, but as she moves towards kitchen door, dish in hands, the tears are flowing and she is howling noisily.*

As she approaches the connecting door, there is a ring at the back door bell and a cheery voice calls "Milk-O!" The back door opens and the MILKMAN *comes chirpily into the kitchen, carrying a pint bottle of milk. The* MILKMAN *is a handsome young man of twenty-six, dressed in white from head to foot. At the back of his head is a white, peaked cap, with the words "Purity Dairies Ltd." on the band. His hair is a mass of curls and his face is sunburnt*)

MILKMAN (*calling happily as he puts the bottle on the table*) Milk-O!

(*It is at this moment that* BARBARA, *dish in hands, passes through into the kitchen, sobbing at her noisiest*)

(*Aghast as he sees her*) Why—Mrs—Martin!

BARBARA (*gurgling with misery*) Oh—Milk-man!

(BARBARA *dazedly puts the dish on the table then totters towards* MILKMAN, *and to his utter astonishment, throws herself up against him and sobs on his chest*)

MILKMAN (*not horrified, but amazed*) Why—Mrs Mar-tin—!

(BARBARA'S *sobbing intensifies. The* MILKMAN *stands for a moment or two, nonplussed. Then, as he becomes really aware of the nearness of Barbara, he, almost nervously, begins to show that he likes it*)

(*Falteringly; soothingly*) There, there, Mrs Martin. (*He is about to stroke her hair, but nervously withdraws his hand*)

BARBARA (*unconsciously snuggling closer to him putting her downstage hand on his shoulder and sobbing*) O-ooo-oooh!

(*The* MILKMAN *stands embarrassed for a moment or two longer. Then, plucking up courage, he sniffs Barbara's hair, and at last, strokes it, then puts his cheek against it*)

MILKMAN (*softly, happily*) There, there, Mrs Martin! (*He takes her hand gently and slips it round his neck. More quietly still*) There, there, Mrs Martin! (*His upstage hand appears round Barbara's waist*) And there, Mrs Martin!

(*They stand thus for a moment, then the* MILKMAN *begins to sway gently to and fro, soothingly, with* BARBARA *in his arms, held very close*)

(*Almost cooing*) There, there, Mrs Martin!

(BARBARA'S *sobbing has almost ceased. It now stops altogether, and after a little while, she gives what can only be described as, a contented purr. A moment or two later the* MILKMAN *follows suit! After which they snuggle closer together and continue swaying*)

BARBARA (*at last, without moving her head, in a tearful voice*) I'm so unhappy.

MILKMAN (*after a quick look down at her head*) I'm sure you are, ma'am.

BARBARA. Otherwise I'd never have dreamed of . . .

MILKMAN. 'Course you wouldn't. Don't think about it, ma'am.

(*They are still swaying*)

BARBARA (*after a while*) We shouldn't be doing this.

MILKMAN. No, ma'am.

BARBARA. It's very wrong, isn't it?

MILKMAN (*murmuring*) According to my boss, the customer's always right!

BARBARA (*after another silence; raising her head, with just a suggestion of tears in her voice*) I think I'm better now. (*She makes to draw away*)

MILKMAN. P'raps you ought to make certain. (*He draws her close again*) I'm in no hurry!

(*They sway again*)

BARBARA (*at last, moving a step away; reluctantly*) Yes, I—I—er— I think I'm better now.

MILKMAN. Just as you say, ma'am. But—(*His arms go out invitingly*) —if you've any doubt . . . !

BARBARA (*almost unconsciously moving back into his arms*) I haven't.

MILKMAN (*as they snuggle up again*) No, ma'am. (*He hesitates then kisses the top of her head*)

BARBARA (*at long last; with more determination, drawing away and dabbing her eyes with her handkerchief*) Well, now—er . . .

(*They look at each other embarrassed*)

Er . . . thank you, milkman.

MILKMAN (*almost as if in a trance*) Don't mention it, ma'am.

BARBARA. I'm sorry if I . . . You *do* understand, don't you?

MILKMAN. Sure, ma'am!

BARBARA. It was just that I—I—I was so upset. I didn't realize what I was . . . You've been a great comfort, milkman.

MILKMAN. Happy to oblige, ma'am. *Any* time you . . . (*He coughs discreetly*)

(*There is an awkward pause*)

BARBARA (*at last—feebly, not knowing quite how to dismiss him*) Yes—

er—well—er—I *think* that will be all, thank you. (*She smiles feebly at him*)

Milkman. Sure, ma'am? (*His arms go half out again, invitingly*)

(Barbara *finds herself in his arms again. They sway gently.* Basil *appears at the french windows. He looks into room, then steps into it and calls*)

Basil (*hesitantly*) Babs, darling—are you there?

(Barbara *and the* Milkman *move apart.* Basil *gives a quick glance towards the kitchen, but then moves into the hall and off upstairs.* Barbara *and the* Milkman *stand still until Basil has disappeared*)

Milkman (*quietly, but* not *alarmed*) Mr Martin?
Barbara (*with a nod of the head*) Yes.
Milkman (*thoughtfully*) H'mm! (*He sighs heavily*) Ah, well . . . !
(*Pulling himself together and speaking reluctantly*) Good morning, ma'am.
(*He backs towards door*)
Barbara (*reluctantly and softly*) Good morning . . . Milkman.

(*The* Milkman, *eyes still on Barbara, backs through the kitchen door, closing it after him.* Barbara *stands for a moment with her eyes on the closed door. She then moves slowly to the table, and almost unconsciously picks up the bottle of milk and holds it close to her with both hands, facing front. She stands quite still for a moment or two, then looks slowly down at the bottle. She lets out a wail of anguish*)

(*Wailing*) I must be going out of my mind! (*The slightest pause*) I meant to order another couple of pints!

QUICK CURTAIN

ACT II

SCENE I

SCENE—*The same. Mid-morning, the same day.*

When the CURTAIN *rises,* BARBARA, *wearing a head-scarf, is hoovering the carpet down* LC. *The room is much tidier. After a moment the telephone rings. She switches off the cleaner, moves up* L *to the desk and lifts the receiver.*

BARBARA (*into the phone*) Brighton five-nine-six-seven-five . . . Yes, it . . . (*With a sudden expression of extreme pleasure mingled with concern*) Oh!—er—hello! . . . (*She looks swiftly towards the hall. Quickly and almost sentimentally*) No, no, not at all. It's—er—quite all right. As a matter of fact I was going to ring *you.* (*Then quickly*) I mean I was going to ring the Dairy. I forgot to . . . What's that? You forgot what? . . . The money? What money? . . . Oh—Oh, yes, of course! How stupid of me! Of course I always settle on Saturday, don't I? (*She almost giggles, then*) I'm so sorry, but I was so upset —I forgot completely . . . Thank you. I'm much better now . . . Shall you what? I didn't quite catch that . . . (*Then almost too eagerly*) Oh, yes, by all means do. I'll—I'll have it ready for you. You're quite sure it's no trouble? . . . (*The reply makes her smile happily to herself*) Well—er—what time will you be—er—calling? . . . At the end of your round. And—er—about what time will that be? . . . Twelve o'clock. (*Eagerly*) Oh, yes, yes. *Quite* convenient! I'll see that it is! (*Then quickly*) Oh, and would you mind bringing two pints extra. I—er—I forgot to ask for them when you—er—when you called this morning. Yes. (*With a far-away sigh*) Two pints . . . Thank you—thank you—er(*rather embarrassed*)—Good-bye! (*She holds the receiver in her hand for a moment looking at it sentimentally, then slowly replaces it on the hook. She then moves slowly into the room, her thoughts miles away. Eventually she moves to the radio* L *and switches it on, then moves dreamily towards the Hoover*)

(*The radio fades in and an orchestra is heard playing "Plaisir d'Amour".* BARBARA *listens dreamily, then unconsciously her hands go on the top of the shaft of the Hoover, and her chin goes on her hands, which, of course, causes her posterior to project outwards slightly. In this undignified position she manages to sway sentimentally to the music as she hums the tune.* BASIL, *wearing a very smart suit and gay tie, comes down the stairs and is about to enter the room, but stops short on seeing Barbara swaying. He gapes at her—unseen by Barbara—then, after a moment, gives a noisy cough and comes into the room.* BARBARA, *on hearing the cough, starts, then showing her annoyance, goes to radio and switches it off*)

BASIL (*curiously; looking at her*) You all right?
BARBARA (*coldly*) With reservations, yes. (*She unplugs the Hoover and winds the flex around the shaft*)
BASIL (*moving above the settee*) Finished?
BARBARA. What?
BASIL. Hoovering.
BARBARA. I have.
BASIL. Good!
BARBARA. I see no cause for elation.
BASIL (*moving up* c) I am not elating. But I loathe trying to talk with that damn thing buzzing in my earhole. (*He searches for his pipe in the shelves above the table*)
BARBARA (*muttering*) So vulgar! (*She begins to push Hoover below the settee towards kitchen*) What are you searching for?
BASIL. My pipe, dammit!
BARBARA. It isn't in here.
BASIL. Blast! (*He moves quickly above the settee, getting in front of the door and facing her*) Barbara, look at me!
BARBARA (*stopping and, after a moment, speaking*) I'm looking.

(BASIL *revolves slowly*)

BASIL (*after a slight pause*) Well?
BARBARA (*after another slight pause*) Well?
BASIL (*impatiently*) Well—how do I look?
BARBARA. Disgusting as usual. Why?
BASIL. Haven't you even noticed that I'm wearing my new suit?
BARBARA. I noticed a dismal "something" about you.
BASIL (*stung*) Babs! (*Muttering*) You'll be sorry . . .
BARBARA. I *am* sorry . . .
BASIL. Thank you!
BARBARA. . . . for the suit! What chance has it got?

(BARBARA *waves him aside and passes through into the kitchen.* BASIL *follows her*)

BASIL (*indignantly*) Now, look here . . . !
BARBARA (*as she wheels Hoover to the corner by the fridge*) I've looked once. There's a limit to human endurance!
BASIL (*following at her heels; almost gibbering*) Barbara—my darling . . .
BARBARA (*crossing below him to the dresser*) Don't "my darling" me! (*She gets a duster from a drawer and returns into the living-room*)
BASIL (*following at her heels*) But . . .
BARBARA. Go on! Out you go! (*Crossing above the settee to dust the mantelpiece*) Go and join your seedy friends down on the beach or in whatever pub you've arranged to meet them. Don't mind me!
BASIL (*following to above the coffee-table*) I am not meeting my seedy friends—(*Quickly*)—I mean George and Delia.
BARBARA. Then why the fancy dress?

BASIL. If you must know . . .

BARBARA (*witheringly*) I can't wait to be told!

BASIL (*moving to* R *of her*) I'm going down to the Theatre Royal, to see Faith Brantingham.

BARBARA (*blinking*) The actress?

BASIL. Yes.

BARBARA. So! (*She crosses in front of him to dust the dining-table and chairs*)

BASIL. Yes. (*He follows to* L *of her*)

BARBARA. Well, well! And when was *this* arranged?

BASIL. It wasn't arranged at all. I'm going down on the off-chance that she'll see me. I phoned the theatre and they said she would be there at eleven.

BARBARA. Well, off you go.

BASIL. Don't you even want to know why I want to see her?

BARBARA. Knowing Faith Brantingham's reputation, I can think of only one reason—and it won't bear talking about. (*Turning*) Out of my way, please. (*She crosses below him to the armchair* L)

BASIL. I'm going to try and persuade her to do my play. Herbert Henkins has sent it to her to read.

BARBARA. She can read, can she? I should never have thought it!

BASIL (*moving* L *of the settee and below it to* R) Now don't start getting snooty about Faith Brantingham. We'll be darned lucky if she does do the play. She's one of the biggest box-office attractions in the country. I mean to say—forty-one—nineteen—thirty-six!

BARBARA (*turning to him; frigidly*) I beg your pardon?

BASIL. Er—her—vital statistics.

BARBARA (*dusting the shelves up* LC) And since when have you developed an interest in women's vital statistics?

BASIL (*moving above the sofa*) I haven't. I'm only interested in Faith Brantingham's.

BARBARA. *What?*

BASIL. You know perfectly well what I mean.

BARBARA. I hope I do! Will you be back to lunch?

BASIL. Of course.

BARBARA. And George and Delia—will they be back too?

BASIL. Of . . . (*He is going to say "of course" but thinks better of it*) Well—er—that was the arrangement,' wasn't it?

BARBARA. Yours and theirs. It certainly wasn't mine. And after that charming little scene at breakfast I wonder they have the nerve to sit down to a meal in this house again.

BASIL. Now don't let's go over all that. Delia apologized for her behaviour.

BARBARA (*moving above the settee*) If Delia apologized for her very existence . . . (*She waves him out of her way again, and moves to the shelves down* R *of the living-room*)

BASIL (*moving* L *of the settee; almost bleating*) I'm sure that with a little co-operation . . .

BARBARA (*dusting*) From whom?

BASIL (*moving below the settee*) Well, all of us.

BARBARA. I want no co-operation from George or Delia, thank you very much. But *you* can start co-operating right away. Have you pencil and paper on you?

BASIL. Yes.

BARBARA. Right. Then take these down. I want you to get them on your way back from your assignation with Faith Brantingham.

BASIL. Now, look . . . !

BARBARA (*practically*) A tin of luncheon meat.

BASIL (*aghast*) What's *that* for?

BARBARA (*shortly*) Luncheon.

BASIL (*aghast*) What? But we've always said we wouldn't have tinned . . .

BARBARA (*inexorably*) A tin of luncheon meat.

(BASIL *sits* L *on the settee*)

BASIL (*writing on the back of an envelope; miserably*) A tin of . . .

BARBARA. A tin of soup.

BASIL (*miserably*) What kind?

BARBARA. Brown Windsor.

BASIL (*flinching*) Brown . . .

BARBARA. A tin of vegetable salad.

BASIL. Oh, God!

BARBARA. A tin of plums!

BASIL. Babs . . . !

BARBARA. And a tin-opener.

BASIL (*gibbering*) You can't do this to me. You know how I loathe anything out of a tin. And what will George and Delia think?

BARBARA. Delia can't—and George can only just, and what he thinks is not of the slightest interest to me. But if *you* think I'm going to spend the next fourteen days slaving over a hot stove you're sadly mistaken.

BASIL (*looking dolefully at the list*) Is that the lot? What if they're in for an evening meal?

BARBARA (*dusting vigorously*) Then you'd better get two tins of each!

BASIL (*in horror*) Oh, no! What about milk?

(BARBARA *stops dead, a dreamy look in her eyes*)

Have you plenty, or shall I get some more?

BARBARA (*very sentimentally*) Milk! (*She stands as if in a trance*)

BASIL. Yes.

BARBARA (*romantically*) Milk! . . . *Milk!* (*She starts singing "Plaisir d'Amour" and waltzing below the settee to the mantelpiece*)

BASIL (*now aware of Barbara's odd behaviour*) Eh? What on earth . . . ? (*Gaping at her*) Babs! (*He rises to above the coffee-table*) I say,

Babs? Are you all right? (*He follows Barbara around, trying to face her, and finds himself waltzing too*) Babs, for goodness' sake!

BARBARA (*stopping waltzing by the armchair; vaguely*) What?

BASIL. What's up, old girl?

BARBARA (*still vaguely*) Nothing, old man.

BASIL (*babbling*) But—but—I mean to say! Suddenly careering round the room like a Swan Lake—I mean a dying swan . . . ! And right in the middle of a conversation about—about—milk!

BARBARA (*the word hits her again*) Milk! (*Again she begins to hum "Plaisir d'Amour" and to waltz, above the settee to the connecting door*)

BASIL (*now thoroughly alarmed*) Babs!

(BARBARA *stops waltzing, but the dreamy look is still in her eyes. She looks at Basil for a moment before speaking*)

BARBARA (*at last*) Why don't you—run along?

BASIL (*moving above the settee and looking at her hard*) I think I will—to the doctor's.

BARBARA (*with a start*) Don't be silly. I'm perfectly all right.

BASIL (*passing her across him to below the settee*) Then I wish you'd behave as if you were. You'd better sit down for a while. Shall I get you a whisky—or brandy or something? (*He moves to the drinks down* R)

BARBARA (*dreamily*) Milk!

BASIL (*blinking*) Eh?

BARBARA (*suddenly irritated*) Oh, do go away, Basil. I can't bear you buzzing round me like a demented bluebottle.

BASIL (*indignantly*) Well, really, I must say . . .

BARBARA (*pushing him up towards the hall door*) Off you go to your Brantingham woman. (*She moves towards the kitchen*)

BASIL (*rather flattered*) I do believe you're jealous!

BARBARA (*her mind on her "milkman"*) Jealous? (*Looking at him with a far-away look of pity*) Silly little man!

BASIL (*stung*) Little!

(BARBARA *has begun to hum and waltz again, into the kitchen*)

(*Suddenly shouting*) Is there anything else you want from the shops?

BARBARA (*waltzing down* R *to the fridge*) Nothing. (*She waltzes back to the living-room*)

BASIL. Then I'm off. I've had just about as much as I can stand of . . .

BARBARA (*standing still*) You've got that list?

BASIL. I have. (*Looking at it, disgustedly*) And I'll be ashamed to give such an order. (*Reading*) Tin of luncheon meat. Tin of soup. Tin of plums. Pah! (*He moves towards the hall*)

BARBARA (*smiling*) What time will you be back?

BASIL. I told George and Delia lunch is at one.

BARBARA (*pointing to Basil's envelope*) Then see you're back with *those* by five minutes to.

BASIL (*miserably*) O.K.
BARBARA. And not a minute before!
BASIL. Eh?
BARBARA. I mean—not a minute later.
BASIL. Oh! (*He goes into the hall*)
BARBARA. Er—have you any idea just how long you *will* be?
BASIL (*returning*) Not really. Why? Does it matter?
BARBARA (*firmly*) Yes—very much.
BASIL (*puzzled*) What?
BARBARA. I should like to know that you—and George—*and* Delia were out of the house until, at least, half-past twelve.
BASIL. Why? Somebody coming to see you?
BARBARA (*somewhat confused*) I—I—I just feel that the less I see of you—and George—*and* Delia today, the happier I shall be! Now—(*with a kittenish wave of the hands*)—run along. Run along!
BASIL (*irritably*) Who the hell do you think I am? Gordon Pirie?

(BASIL *is about to go when the telephone rings*)

I'll answer it! (*He goes to the telephone and lifts the receiver*)

(BARBARA *goes into the kitchen, shakes the duster out of the back door, and puts it in its drawer*)

Brighton five-nine-six-seven-five. Yes? . . . George! What the . . . ? . . . What? I can't hear a word you're saying. You're spluttering . . . Get what ready? . . . Blankets, hot-water bottles? What the hell's wrong? . . . But you've got to explain. You can't just . . . Surprise? Damn your surprises. Barbara will want to know . . . George, for God's sake! . . . Delia? No, she isn't here . . . Isn't she with you? . . . George, what has happened . . . But you've *got* to stop! . . . George . . George . . . (*He rattles receiver hook*) Damn and blast! (*He puts receiver down*)

(BARBARA *comes back into the living-room*)

BARBARA. Who was it?
BASIL (*wincing*) George.
BARBARA. George? (*Hopefully*) Are they having lunch out?
BASIL (*wretchedly, not knowing how to tell her*) Babs, darling . . .
BARBARA. H'm! Obviously they're *not*. Well, what did he want?
BASIL (*moving to R of her; timorously*) Blankets. Hot-water bottles.
BARBARA (*almost a yelp*) What? *Blankets* . . . ?
BASIL (*almost gibbering*) Babs—sweetheart . . .
BARBARA (*trying to control herself*) What is it? What's happened? Oh, God, don't say Delia really has got scarlet fever?
BASIL. It isn't Delia. (*He moves L to the armchair*)
BARBARA. Then who?
BASIL (*muttering dazedly*) Blankets. Hot-water bottles.
BARBARA. You mean something's happened to George? (*Moving*

to L *of him*) For heaven's sake, man, don't just stand there mumbling, tell me what's wrong. He isn't dead, is he?

BASIL (*still dazed*) He didn't *say* he was. (*He sits in the armchair*)

BARBARA (*exasperated*) Then what . . . ?

BASIL. Blankets. Hot-water bottles!

BARBARA. Basil Martin—before I start running up the wall, will you *please* tell me . . .

BASIL. I can't. I don't know.

BARBARA. You don't . . . ?

BASIL. George wouldn't tell me—damn him. Just said it was a surprise!

BARBARA (*exasperatedly*) Surprise? Do you mean it's some joke?

BASIL (*rising and suddenly yelling*) I don't know! I don't know! But if it is I'll break his blasted neck.

BARBARA (*moving below the settee*) No, you won't. *I* will!

BASIL (*moving in circles down* L) Blankets—hot-water bottles!

(BARBARA *gives a loud groan and covers her face with her hands*)

BARBARA (*hollowly*) This is their *first* day! (*Moving to the* R *end of the settee*) And they're here for thirteen more!

BASIL (*moving to* L *of her*) Hadn't we better . . . ?

BARBARA. The hot-water bottles are in the bathroom cupboard. And the blankets . . . And there's no hot water! Those two bagged the lot! That means . . . !

BASIL (*leaping above the settee towards kitchen*) I'll put a kettle on. Don't you upset yourself, Babs, darling.

BARBARA (*sitting* R *on the settee; furiously*) I'm not upsetting *myself* —there's no need! You and George and Delia are doing it very successfully!

BASIL (*moving to the kitchen*) Where did you say the hot-water bottles are?

BARBARA (*shortly; she is almost hysterical, but manages to control herself—just*) In the bathroom cupboard.

BASIL (*running towards the hall*) Which shelf?

BARBARA. There are only two—they're on one of them.

BASIL. And the blankets—don't worry, I'll get them. Where are they?

BARBARA. We're using all our spare ones. They'll have to come off one of the beds.

BASIL. Which bed?

BARBARA (*wildly*) What does it matter, *which* bed? (*Rising to the stairs; with an impatient gesture*) Oh, for heaven's sake! Look! I'll get them! You just go and fill a kettle.

BASIL (*moving towards the kitchen rapidly*) O.K.! (*Turning at kitchen door*) Which kettle?

(BARBARA, *who is just about to go into the hall turns and gives a slightly hysterical whinnying cry, then goes out and up the stairs.* BASIL

*looks after her, helplessly, then goes into the kitchen. He picks up a small
kettle from stove, then a larger one. The front door bell rings)*

(Starting) Oh, no! *Not* already! *(Kettles in hand he rushes from the
kitchen and out into the hall, calling upstairs as he goes)* It's all right,
Babs! I'll go!

(BASIL *exits to the hall and is heard opening and closing the front door.*
DELIA *comes quickly into the room and moves down* R. *She is in a very
distressed state.* BASIL *follows, still with the kettles, to down* C)

Delia—what . . . ?

(DELIA *bursts into noisy sobbing)*

Delia!

(DELIA *sits* R *on the settee and pummels it with her fists)*

Delia! My *dear!* *(He sits close to her on the settee, then with a quick look
towards the hall, leaps up guiltily, moves to the small chair* L; *puts the kettles
on them, and brings the chair to within a couple of yards of Delia and
distractedly sits—on the kettles. He leaps up again with a small yelp, takes
the kettles in hand and sits facing Delia).* What *has* happened?
DELIA. The end of the world!
BASIL. That's too much to hope for. Now come on—tell me!
DELIA *(whimpering)* George . . . !
BASIL. What about him? He isn't ill, is he?
DELIA. Not yet! He *will* be when I've finished with him!
BASIL. But what . . . ? George phoned me just now. Told me
to get blankets—hot water bottles.
DELIA. He did *what.*
BASIL *(nodding)* Yes. I was just . . . *(He holds out the kettles)*
DELIA. You mean he's bringing her *here?*
BASIL *(leaping up)* Her? Who? *(With a groan)* Oh, no! Not
somebody *else!*
DELIA *(rising and moving up* R *of the settee towards the hall)* I'm going!
BASIL *(chasing after her round* R *of the settee)* Going where?
DELIA. Home—to mother.
BASIL. What? But you can't—not just like that! What will George
say? Delia, what *has* happened?
DELIA *(moving above the settee to* L) The rat! The weazel! The
elephant!
BASIL. George?
DELIA *(nodding vigorously)* The skunk—the snake—the baboon!
BASIL *(moving* R *of her; muttering)* God! What a mixture! *(Des-
perately)* But, Delia, you said something about "bringing her here".
Who—*who's* he bringing?
DELIA *(with a howl)* His wife!
BASIL *(with a yelp)* What?
DELIA *(nodding her head vigorously)* Mmmm!

BASIL (*babbling*) His . . . ! But—but—what are you talking about? You're his wife—or you're going to be!

DELIA. That's what I thought. (*Weeping*) Oh, Basil!

BASIL (*with an attempt at firmness*) Delia, we must get this straight. This—this—wife of George's. Did he *tell* you she was his wife?

DELIA (*moving down* L) He told everybody.

BASIL. Everybody? But—(*Running his hand—with the kettle in it—over his hair*)—I'm going mad! Where did you meet her? Did you run into her on the front?

DELIA (*snivelling*) He fished her out of the sea.

BASIL (*blinking*) Fished her . . . Do you mean she's a—a mermaid?

DELIA (*almost shouting*) He rescued her!

BASIL. Rescued . . .

DELIA. She fell in and he dived in and brought her out!

BASIL (*moving below* R *of the settee; stunned*) Good Lord! (*Babbling*) But did he *know* she was his wife when he went in after her?

DELIA (*irritably*) How do I know?

BASIL. He *couldn't* have done—otherwise he'd have left her there. Where did this happen?

DELIA (*snivelling*) At the end of the Palace Pier. (*Moving* L *of Basil*) There was a crowd watching the fishing. Somebody caught a fish and everybody tried to see it. Then there was a splash and the next thing I knew, there was another splash and George had dived into the water and—when he came back he—he had a wife with him!

BASIL. Did—did she know she had a husband with her?

DELIA. She didn't look as if she cared who she had. That was when George calmly announced that it was all right—that there was no need for alarm and that she was his wife and he was going to take her home!

BASIL. His wife! and—what did you do?

DELIA. I asked him what he was talking about.

BASIL. And what did he say?

DELIA. Told me to get to hell out of it!

BASIL. He didn't! What *did* you do?

DELIA (*sitting on the settee*) I gave him a punch in the stomach he won't forget for a while and got to hell out of it!

BASIL (*moving below her to the fireplace, kettles still in hand*) It's incredible! Did you know he'd been married? I mean had he ever said anything about having had a wife?

DELIA. Not him! The rat, the weazel, the elephant! And now you say he's bringing her here?

BASIL. He must be! The skunk, the snake, the baboon! (*Distractedly*) Heaven help me! *What* am I going to say to Babs?

DELIA (*wildly*) What am I going to say to mother?

BASIL (*wildly*) Damn your mother!

DELIA (*rising and howling*) Basil!

Basil (*moving a pace to* c*; desperately*) I'm sorry Delia, I didn't mean that. I'm very fond of your mother. I mean . . . Oh, what am I talking about? I can't even think straight. When Babs hears about this she'll—she'll really go berserk.

Delia (*moving* c) That'll make two of us—because the moment he brings her through that door . . .

Basil (*with a yelp*) No! (*Moving towards her*) Delia, for heaven's sake . . . have a little consideration for me and what's left of my marital happiness.

Delia (*dissolving into tears*) I—I—loved him, Basil!

Basil (*coming close to her*) Of course you did.

Delia. I worshipped him.

Basil. Of course you did.

Delia. I gave him my all.

Basil. Of course you did. (*Then starting*) I say! You didn't *did* you?

Delia (*nodding her head*) I drew my last five pounds ten out of the Post Office Savings Bank so we could come down here. (*Sobbing on his chest*) What'll I do?

Basil (*muttering*) Ask him for it back.

Delia. Oh, Basil . . .

Basil (*arms—and kettles—round her*) Poor Delia.

(Barbara, *carrying three blankets and two hot-water bottles, comes down the stairs and into the room*)

Barbara (*bitingly*) Hey nonny nonny!

(Basil *leaps away from Delia*)

(*Moving to the kitchen door*) Carry on. Don't mind me!

Basil (*after throwing the kettles on to the floor viciously*) Babs . . . !

Barbara (*looking at the kettles*) That's right! Smash up the happy home! The fun we're having!

Delia (*moving* l *of Barbara; weeping*) Barbara—you don't understand.

(Basil *picks up the kettles*)

Barbara. Maybe not, but shall we say I've got an inkling?

Basil (*desperately*) You haven't! You couldn't have. (*Moving below the settee* l) Nobody could. Oh, how am I going to tell you?

Barbara (*sharply*) In plain English and as quickly as possible.

Basil (*moving down* l) Something terrible's happened.

(Delia *howls and collapses* r *on the settee*)

Barbara (*moving* r *of Basil; coldly*) Go on!

Basil (*gibbering in his misery*) I will. I must! But Barbara . . .

(*He tries to take her in his arms, but* Barbara *puts the blankets in them and steps back*)

. . . when I tell you, I beg you to think, not of this black *today,* but of all our happy yesterdays . . .

BARBARA (*moving away* L*; muttering*) And he wonders why his novels don't sell!

BASIL (*following her, with the blankets*) . . . Our happy yesterdays and all the golden tomorrows that lie ahead.

BARBARA (*sitting* L *on the settee*) You offered me brandy ten minutes ago. I should have taken it.

BASIL (*babbling*) Babs . . . George . . .

DELIA. The rat!

BARBARA. What?

BASIL. The skunk, the weazel! (*He moves to the fireplace. He wails*) Oh! *And* to have the nerve to bring her here!

(DELIA *moans*)

BARBARA (*with a puzzled look towards Delia*) Bring her here? Well, if he had sufficient nerve to get engaged to her, I don't see . . .

DELIA (*snapping*) Basil isn't talking about me!

BARBARA (*gaping at her*) Not?

DELIA. No!

BARBARA. But he said "Bring her here . . . " (*Then with horror*) You *mean* . . . ? (*She stiffens, rises and fixes Basil with an icy eye*) Bring—who—here?

BASIL (*a cry from the heart*) Babs—darling . . . (*He drops the kettles and the blankets*)

BARBARA (*relentlessly*) Bring who . . . ?

BASIL. Babs . . . !

BARBARA. Bring . . . ?

BASIL (*unconsciously kneeling, first on the kettles, then on the blankets*) *Beloved*—have mercy . . . !

BARBARA (*her voice trembling with suppressed emotion*) Delia—who—what—is George bringing here?

DELIA. His wife!

BARBARA. His . . . ?

(BASIL, *still on his knees, prostrates himself two or three times, Moslem fashion, and moans loudly as he does so*)

Is this a joke?

DELIA. If it is, *I'm* not laughing!

BARBARA. But George isn't mar . . . !

DELIA (*howling*) He *is*!

BARBARA (*wandering around the small chair to above it, almost clutching the furniture for support*) The blankets—the hot water bottles—they're for her—his wife?

DELIA. Yes.

BARBARA (*almost demented*) No! No! It isn't true—it *can't* be!

DELIA (*gulping*) He saved her from being drowned this morning.

BARBARA. And *married* her?

DELIA. If he did, he did it in the water.
BARBARA. And why is he bringing her here?
BASIL (*weakly*) Perhaps she's dying.
DELIA (*venomously*) If she isn't now, she soon will be!
BARBARA (*moving above* L *of the settee; trying to speak calmly*) Delia, this is my house and any slaughtering to be done in it will be done by me. (*Moving down* L, *glaring at them both*) And I look like having a very busy day! (*She moves* C)
BASIL (*running after Babs on his knees*) Babs—sweetheart! We mustn't lose our heads!
BARBARA. You never *had* yours.
BASIL. Then I'd like to know what's bumping and jumping where it ought to be.
BARBARA (*moving* L *of Delia*) Does this wife know that George is engaged to you?
DELIA. If she doesn't, she's damn well going to!
BARBARA (*with a touch of hysteria*) Of all the sordid, disgusting situations. (*Turning on Basil*) All hell is going to be let loose, you realize that, don't you? And here in our home! We shan't be able to move for dirty linen! (*She moves to the french windows*)
BASIL (*rising*) Babs—darling . . .
BARBARA (*moving* L *of the table up* C) If you "Babs darling" me again I'll hit you, I swear I will.
BASIL (*moving* L *of Barbara*) Babs—darling!

(BARBARA *picks up a small china plate and brandishes it wildly*)

DELIA (*running* R *of the settee to* R *of Barbara; with a shriek*) Babs— darling!

(BARBARA *turns threateningly to Delia*)

(*Terrified*) Aaah!
BARBARA (*realizing what she was about to do*) I must be put away! Somebody, please, put me away! (*She replaces the plate*)

(*The front door bell rings*)

BASIL. Aaah! Is this . . . ?
DELIA (*moving to the front door*) Yes! (*Returning to* R *of Barbara*) There's a taxi at the gate. (*Hysterically*) Barbara, don't let them in!
BARBARA. What?
DELIA. I mean, don't let George bring *her* in.
BARBARA (*snapping*) What do you suggest he should do with her —plant her in the garden?
BASIL (*wandering around to down* L; *almost in a stupor*) "Life is mostly froth and bubble."
BARBARA. What are you babbling about?
BASIL (*miserably*) Bubbles.

(*The door bell rings again*)

BARBARA (*every nerve tingling*) Oooh!

DELIA (*moving below Barbara to* L) I don't want to see her.

BARBARA (*to Delia*) There's no *need* for you to see her. George can take her straight up to bed.

(DELIA *gives an agonized yelp and collapses, weeping, in the armchair*)

BASIL. The hot-water bottles! We haven't . . .

BARBARA (*wildly*) Whose fault is that? (*Looking round room at the blankets, kettles—all on the floor*) And look at this room! Damn George Padstow! *And* his women! (*She rushes around picking up the blankets*) Delia! Don't just stand there! For heaven's sake do something. What will the woman think?

(BASIL *picks up the kettles*)

DELIA. Who cares what she thinks?

(BASIL *moves towards the kitchen*)

BARBARA. I do! I'm not having any woman saying my home . . .

(*The bell rings again*)

Basil! (*She drops the blankets*)

BASIL (*turning*) Yes, dear?

BARBARA. The door! Go and let them in!

BASIL. No, no. I daren't go! I don't know *what* I'd do if *I* went.

BARBARA (*moving upstage*) I know exactly what I should do if *I* did—that's why you're going!

BASIL (*moving towards the hall*) Oh, Lord! Oh, Lord!

BARBARA (*sharply*) Basil!

BASIL (*jumping round, nervously, irritably*) God, how I hate my name!

BARBARA (*moving up to him*) So do I. Unless you're going to hit George over the head with them, you won't want these! (*She snatches the kettles from him and takes them and the bottles into the kitchen*)

(BASIL *goes out into hall and to front door*)

DELIA (*rising and following Barbara into the kitchen*) The minute they come through that door I shall scream, I know I shall.

BARBARA. That'll be a great help! (*She puts the kettles on the stove*)

DELIA. You won't be nice to her, will you?

(BARBARA *returns to the living-room.* DELIA *follows*)

BARBARA. *Nice*! I shall be so nasty I almost pity the woman!

(BARBARA *moves down* L. DELIA *follows.* GEORGE'S *voice is heard off*)

GEORGE (*off*) 'Lo, Bas, old boy. About time! We're here at last. Look—you'd better get a . . . (*His voice is drowned by* DELIA *and* BARBARA *on stage*)

DELIA (*beginning to make odd noises*) I—I'm starting! (*She moves up* LC)

Barbara (*wildly*) Go on! Let it rip! (*She picks up a blanket*)

(Basil *is heard to give something between a cry of horror and a howl off stage*)

(*Hearing this*) What on earth . . . ?

(Basil, *a dazed and horrified look on his face, totters in from the hall, and leans weakly against the wall*)

(*Gaping at him*) Basil, what . . . ?

Basil (*after limply running a hand across his eyes*) Ave Maria! (*He moves down* R *of the settee to down* C)

Barbara. What?

Basil (*pulling himself together with an effort and tottering down towards Barbara*) Donna il Mobile!

Barbara (*furiously*) Basil, for heaven's sake . . . !

(Basil *takes the blanket from Barbara with one hand, and, trailing it along the floor, moves blindly towards the hall again.*

Delia (*nearly hysterical*) Basil, what is it? Is she—is she . . . ?

Basil (*dazedly*) I'll say she is!

Barbara (*running upstage to* L *of Basil; wildly*) Is what?

(Delia *moves* L *of Barbara*)

Basil (*feebly*) Forty-one—nineteen—thirty-six!

Basil *totters out into the hall trailing the blanket, as—*

the Curtain *falls*

Scene 2

Scene—*The same. Half-an-hour later.*

When the Curtain *rises,* Barbara *is in the kitchen,* George *in the lounge. The kitchen table is now filled with packets, basins, spoons, and everything necessary for the preparation of a big meal. Pans are on the cooker, and the whole kitchen gives the impression of being very much in use.* Barbara *is looking in the oven, from which steam is coming. She closes the door, straightens up, wipes her heated brow with the back of her hand, then comes to the table, picks up a basin in which is a mixture, and begins whisking madly, a formidable expression on her face.*

In the living-room, George *is seated* L *on the settee. He is in shirt-sleeves, his coat over the back, and is busy cleaning an entrée dish. One or two other pieces of silver are laid out on the coffee table, which is moved near to him and is covered with newspaper. Some of the items are cleaned, others not—the latter look very dull. A tin of "Silvo" is also on the table. The small chair has been replaced. After polishing furiously for a while*

GEORGE *wipes his heated brow, then continues to work, singing quietly to himself:* "*This is a lovely way to spend an evening*".
DELIA *enters downstairs carrying a tray on which are coffee things for one, and moves above the settee on her way to the kitchen. As she enters,* GEORGE *looks up at her and winks.* DELIA *glares at him murderously.*

GEORGE (*chirpily*) Wotcher! (*Singing and grinning at Delia*) "I never felt more like singing the Blues . . . "

(DELIA *stops, turns and glares at him*)

(*With disdain*) Square!

(DELIA, *exasperated, goes into the kitchen*)

DELIA (*to Barbara; bitingly*) Miss Brantingham doesn't want coffee!
BARBARA (*stopping whisking for a moment; in a voice devoid of any expression*) Miss Brantingham doesn't want coffee.
DELIA. She wants a gin and tonic.
BARBARA (*in the same flat voice*) She wants a gin and tonic.

(DELIA *puts the tray down on the draining-board*)

DELIA. With lemon.
BARBARA. With lemon. (*She goes to the dresser for a lemon and returns to the table*)
DELIA. What shall I do?
BARBARA. Take Miss Brantingham a gin and tonic—(*Handing her the whole lemon*)—with lemon. (*She whisks furiously*)
DELIA (*timorously*) Barbara . . .

(*The front door bell rings*)

BARBARA (*sharply*) There's someone at the front door.
DELIA. But . . .
BARBARA. See who it is, will you?
DELIA (*turning towards the connecting door; muttering*) I've only one pair of hands.
BARBARA. That's all you need.

(DELIA, *still clutching the lemon, goes into the living-room. The bell rings again*)

DELIA (*bitingly to George*) Can't you hear the front door bell? (*She moves down* R *of the settee*)
GEORGE (*polishing furiously*) Yes, can't you?
DELIA (*moving past him below the settee*) Why don't you answer it?
GEORGE (*chirpily*) Only got one pair of hands. (*He pats her posterior lightly as she passes him*)
DELIA (*moving towards the hall*) Yes, and with *their* nasty habits—*they're* one pair too many!

(*The bell rings again*)

(*Shouting towards the hall*) Oh, shut up!

(DELIA *goes out into the hall towards the front door.* BASIL, *with a large basket on his arm, comes quickly into the kitchen through the back door. He looks hopefully towards Barbara*)

BASIL (*timorously*) Hello—I'm back. (*Wiping his brow*) Phew! It's hot out! Must be pretty near the seventies.

(BARBARA *glares at him*)

Er—chicken smells good. (*A slight pause*) I—I think I've got everything.

(BASIL *puts the basket on the table after sweeping several things to one side. Just in time,* BARBARA *saves one or two things from falling to the floor*)

(*Gulping*) Sorry! (*Taking a parcel from basket rapidly and opening it*) Smoked salmon. (*Nervously*) Devil of a price. Seventeen shillings for that! (*He holds out the open parcel for Barbara to see.*)

(BARBARA *clutches the table, for support. She then, numbly, takes the parcel from him with both hands and moves away from the table, gaping at the expensive slices, hypnotized*)

BASIL (*as he produces them*) Olives—cocktail biscuits—two bottles of Graves. I hope she likes *white* wine.
BARBARA (*almost croaking*) She won't. (*She puts the salmon on a plate*) She'll like red.
BASIL (*trying to laugh*) Oh, not with chicken, darling, surely?
BARBARA (*hollowly*) Surely. (*Her eyes return to the salmon*)
BASIL (*still apprehensively*) Oh, and I got a half bottle of Grand Marnier. (*Taking it from the basket*) I—I thought, while I was *at* it . . . (*He looks towards Barbara nervously*)
BARBARA (*weakly*) . . . you might as well get *on* with it.
BASIL (*gulping*) Er—yes.
BARBARA. And you *did*.
BASIL (*coming to her; desperately*) Babs—my darling—I *know* how you feel.

(BARBARA *gives a sudden loud and abrupt whinney*)

(*Gulping*) I know it was a damn silly idea of George's . . .
BARBARA. It was . . .
BASIL (*eagerly*) But darling, it *might* come off. And if it *does* . . . !
BARBARA (*her eyes still on the salmon*) And if it *doesn't* . . . ! Well, I suppose it'll be something to look back on—the day we had olives, Grand Marnier, Faith Brantingham and smoked salmon for lunch! (*She moves to the fridge and puts the salmon in*)
BASIL (*taking the bottles of wine to the fridge*) These had better go in too.

(BARBARA *puts the wine in the fridge.* DELIA, *enters from the hall carrying a large and expensive-looking suitcase, across the downstage side of which is plastered a large slip of paper bearing in bold letters the name* MISS FAITH BRANTINGHAM. *She moves to the kitchen*)

GEORGE (*as Delia passes above him; looking at suitcase*) Cheerio! Have a good time!

(DELIA, *ignoring him sweeps off into kitchen*)

DELIA (*in the kitchen*) This has arrived!

BARBARA (*turning and eyeing the case, seeing the large lettering*) I should say it belongs to Miss Faith Brantingham.

DELIA. They've sent it up from her hotel.

BARBARA (*to Basil*) Is she moving in for the summer?

BASIL (*wretchedly*) George rang the hotel. It's her clothes—she had to have fresh ones; her others are soaked. Dammit, she couldn't sit down to lunch stark naked.

BARBARA (*moving above the kitchen table*) Given the opportunity, I wouldn't mind betting . . . (*To Delia*) You'd better take them up to her, hadn't you?

DELIA (*in a high-pitched complaining voice*) Why do I have to do all the chasing after her?

BARBARA. I'm sure George would be only too happy to oblige.

DELIA (*sulkily*) What about her gin and tonic?

BARBARA. Oh, yes! Basil, Miss Brantingham pooh-pooh's morning coffee.

BASIL. Oh? Does she?

BARBARA. She does. She favours gin and tonic.

BASIL. Oh!

DELIA (*holding out the lemon*) With lemon.

BARBARA. You'd better fix her one, hadn't you?

BASIL. Come on, Delia. I'll get it.

(BASIL, *with an anxious look at Barbara, goes into the living-room*)

DELIA. Phew! This kitchen's like an oven!

(BARBARA *reacts to this.* DELIA, *with the suitcase, follows Basil into the living-room.* BASIL *goes to the drinks shelves down* R *and takes out bottles and glasses.* BARBARA *returns to her work in the kitchen*)

GEORGE (*to Delia, after a quick look at suitcase*) Did you have good weather? (*He roars with laughter, then, seeing Basil with bottles*) Ah! Drinkey-boos! Just what the doctor ordered. And am I ready for one! Ruddy warm today!

BASIL (*turning angrily*) George . . . ! (*He shrugs his shoulders and pours gin into two glasses. He also opens two small tonics*) Get me a tray, Delia.

(DELIA *puts down the suitcase, crosses* L *takes a small silver tray from the coffee-table*)

GEORGE (*protesting*) Oi! I've just cleaned that! Needn't bother about a tray for me.

(DELIA *moves back to* L *of Basil*)

BASIL (*after a glare at George*) Oh . . . lemon!

(DELIA *holds out the lemon*)

GEORGE (*blithely*) No lemon for me, old man. I like to taste the gin.

BASIL (*after another glare at George's back*) Get me a knife, will you, Delia?

(DELIA *gives a little whimper, then moves to the kitchen door and goes through it*)

DELIA (*in the kitchen*) A knife.

(BASIL *takes a gin and tonic to George, who murmers "Thanks"*)

BARBARA. What?

(BASIL *returns to the drinks*)

DELIA. I want a knife.

(GEORGE *takes a swig and resumes polishing*)

BARBARA (*after a look at her*) You must find some other way—that's too messy!

(BASIL *prepares another drink and sets out glasses*)

DELIA (*exasperatedly*) Basil wants a knife to cut the lemon.
BARBARA (*getting a small knife from the dresser and giving it to Delia*) By the way, how's she looking?
DELIA. Who?
BARBARA. The Brantingham woman, of course.
DELIA. I haven't so much as glanced at her.
BARBARA. That was clever of you, considering the amount of her there is!

(DELIA *returns into the living-room, and takes the knife to Basil*)

BASIL (*taking the knife*) Thanks. (*He slices the lemon and drops a slice into glass on tray*) There we are, Delia.

(DELIA *takes the tray, then moves to the suitcase and picks it up*)

GEORGE (*cheerfully*) And—Duckie . . .

(DELIA *turns and looks at him coldly*)

Don't forget . . . service with a smile!

(DELIA, *almost snorting, exits into the hall and upstairs*)

Something tells me Delia isn't exactly entering into the spirit of our little plot.

BASIL (*looking towards the kitchen*) And *I* don't *need* telling that somebody else isn't either! (*Moving above the settee to* L) And for the Lord's sake don't call it "our" plot. It was yours entirely. And if you don't mind my saying so, George . . .

GEORGE. It stinks. Is that what you think?

BASIL. It's certainly a little "high"!

GEORGE (*cheerfully*) Cheer up, old boy! Everything's going to work out fine—you'll see! Bas, old boy, before the day's out you'll be down on your *knees* . . .

BASIL (*looking towards the kitchen*) I *have* been already, and a lot of good it did!

GEORGE. I mean in *gratitude* to *me*.

BASIL. I wish I could share your beautiful optimism!

GEORGE. But, good Lord, old boy, the woman can't *refuse* to read your play now.

BASIL (*irritably*) Why can't she?

GEORGE. Well, not if she's got any sense of decency at all. I mean to say—you're *my friend* . . .

BASIL (*still irritably*) Well?

GEORGE. And, dash it all, *I did* pull her out of the sea!

BASIL. Yes! After you'd bloody well pushed her *in*!

GEORGE (*slightly alarmed*) Sssh! Not so loud! We don't want her to know that do we? (*He points to the ceiling*)

BASIL. How you managed it without anyone seeing you . . .

GEORGE. You've got to be clever about these things.

BASIL (*with a grunt*) Huh! (*He moves to the fireplace*) I wish you'd been a bit cleverer and not let Delia come back here in hysterics, thinking you were married to the woman.

GEORGE. What else could I do? I had to get her away before anyone tumbled to it that she was Faith Brantingham, *and* before she'd begun to come to her senses. So I just dragged her hair over her face, flung my jacket over her—statistics, told everybody she was my wife and—well, interest waned!

BASIL. But didn't she want to know where you were taking her—in the taxi, I mean?

GEORGE. She didn't seem to care. She was too intent on showing her gratitude.

BASIL (*with a look at him*) That *could* mean *anything*, of course.

GEORGE (*polishing a vase*) It could've—if it'd been a longer journey.

BASIL (*still with irritation*) But knowing Barbara isn't feeling—er—at her best this morning—to ask the woman to stay for lunch . . . !

GEORGE (*with slight impatience*) Well, good Lord, we didn't want her clearing off ten minutes after she'd arrived, did we—not after all the trouble I'd gone to get her here? That was the whole idea—get her under your roof, fuss over her in bed . . .

BASIL. I beg your pardon?

GEORGE (*waving his hand irritably*) . . . get her in a receptive mood, give her a slap-up lunch, and after that . . . And, dash it all, we were going to *have* lunch in any case, weren't we?

BASIL (*muttering*) Yes. But it wasn't going to be *quite* so *slap-up!*

(DELIA *comes downstairs and into the room, carrying the tray with the empty glass and bottle on it*)

BASIL (*seeing her; anxiously*) Everything O.K., Delia?

DELIA (*moving above the settee; glaring*) You don't mean with *me*, do you?

BASIL (*irritably*) Did Miss Brantingham say anything?

DELIA (*flatly*) Yes.

BASIL. What?

DELIA (*holding out the tray*) She'd like another.

BASIL (*moving* L *of Delia*) Good Lord! (*He takes the tray, moves below her to the drinks, and prepares another gin and tonic*)

DELIA (*coming down to* L *of George*) Great idea this of yours, wasn't it?

GEORGE. What's wrong with it, Duckie?

DELIA. Nothing! Nothing at all! (*Moving below the settee as she speaks*) Except that, at the rate she's going, and by the time you and Basil can get round to talking about his play, she's going to be so pickled, plastered and "pi-eyed", she won't know whether she's coming, going, or *been*, or whether she said "Good-bye" before she went!

(DELIA *snatches the tray from Basil and goes out and up the stairs again*)

BASIL (*moving to the hall and looking nervously towards the staircase*) She'll have milk next time, and like it!

(*The telephone rings*)

(*Starting nervously*) Aah! Oh, God! (*Moving to the desk*) My nerves! (*He lifts the receiver*) Yes . . . Who? . . . (*Staring*) Oh—er—just a minute! (*Turning to George apprehensively*) It's some fellow from the theatre asking about—(*he indicates upstairs*) What shall I . . . ?

GEORGE (*rising; easily*) Leave it to me. (*He puts down his polishing and goes to the phone*)

(BASIL *moves to the french windows*)

Hullo, yes . . . ? No, this isn't Miss Brantingham . . . (*He smirks towards Basil*) . . . Who? . . . Oh, yes . . . How nice. How *very* nice of you, old boy! Oh, she's—not too bad—bit wiffly-waffly you know . . . Can you what? . . . Come up and see her . . . Well—er—she's resting at the moment—in bed . . . What's that? You don't *mind!* No, I daresay not, old man, but, will *she?* . . . What did you say? "Not on your Nelly". . . I get you! Well, if you'll hang on a moment I'll see if she's feeling that way inclined.

Hang on, will you? (*He puts the receiver down on the desk and crosses back to his silver, sitting and picking up the vase again, giving it a final rub*)

BASIL (*gaping at him*) What . . . ? (*He moves to* L *of George*)

GEORGE (*explaining casually*) Her leading man. Wants to know how she is, and can he come up and see her.

BASIL. Well . . . ?

GEORGE. He can't. (*Admiring his vase*) Now *that* with half a dozen roses in it'll look smashing in the middle of the table.

BASIL (*after an embarrassed look towards the telephone*) We haven't got half a dozen roses—we haven't got one. (*Muttering*) There are the hollyhocks of course . . . (*He moves back to the french windows*)

GEORGE. Pity! Ah well, never mind. (*Surveying the silver*) Well, that seems to be the lot!

BASIL (*looking towards the telephone*) Look, what about . . . ?

GEORGE (*easily*) Oh, yes! (*He crosses back to the phone and picks up receiver*) Hello, you there? . . . Good! . . . Well, Miss Branting-ham says how sweet of you to 'phone . . . and she'd simply *love* you to call . . . (*Quickly and firmly*) Wait for it! She'd *love* you to call, but she won't hear of you wasting your time . . . H'm? You wouldn't be wasting your . . . ? (*With relish*) Oh, yes, you would, duckie! . . . No, no! Nothing at all . . . she has every-thing she wants . . . yes . . . yes . . . (*Suddenly*) Half a minute though! As you're not coming to see her, how about sending her a few flowers? (*He winks at Basil*) A few roses, say! About a dozen. That should fill the vase—I mean the bill. (*Covering the mouthpiece and speaking quickly to Basil*) What colour?

BASIL (*hoarsely*) Red! (*He moves down* L)

GEORGE (*into the phone*) Red ones. A dozen red roses. Wouldn't that be nice . . . ? (*Agreeing*) you *will* . . . ? I *thought* you would. They say there's one born every . . . I mean . . . I'll see she gets them right away. (*Happily*) Bye-bye, now! (*He replaces the receiver and comes back to the silver*) Well, that's the flower problem settled! (*He sits* L *on the settee*)

(DELIA *comes down the stairs and into the room, carrying a flimsy, but expensive-looking summer dress. She is near to hysteria again*)

DELIA (*as she comes down* C) Ooooh!

BASIL (*starting and going towards her*) Delia!

DELIA (*fuming*) Don't talk to me! Don't even speak to me.

GEORGE (*calmly*) Steady as she goes, old girl!

(BASIL *sits down* L)

DELIA (*rolling the dress up into a bundle savagely*) Aaaah!

(BARBARA *hears Delia and comes through connecting door*)

I'm supposed to be on holiday—(*to George*)—do you realize that? And I'm just working my fingers to the bone running after that . . . that *trollop!*

BARBARA (*moving down* R; *coldly*) Now, what . . . ?

DELIA (*fuming*) Now what? I'll tell you *now what!* Not only do I have to unpack her bag for her, but will I get her dress ironed, if you please! *Pretty,* isn't it?

GEORGE (*indicating the dress*) Is it? Let's have a look at it!

DELIA (*hurling the dress, which is now in a ball, into his lap*) You can look at it, and you can damn well iron it!

BARBARA (*sharply*) Don't talk nonsense, Delia. You'll have to. do it!

DELIA (*fuming*) Why will I? I'm not getting anything out of this? It's all George's crazy idea. Well, let him get on with it!

GEORGE (*as he lets the dress fall open*) Now, listen, duckie, I don't want to smack your bottom in public, but . . . (*Looking at dress admiringly*) I say! (*He gives a wolf-whistle*) Kinda nifty, isn't it— what there is of it!

BARBARA. Come and get the things, Delia. You'll have to iron it in here. I can't do with you in the kitchen.

(BARBARA *returns into the kitchen*)

DELIA (*moving above the settee; almost speechless*) This is the last thing I do if . . . If it's the last thing I do! (*She goes into kitchen after Barbara*)

(BARBARA *gets the ironing-board from above the fridge, and the iron from the dresser, during the following*)

GEORGE (*holding the dress up at arm's length and eyeing it with relish; almost growling*) Mmmm!

BASIL (*rising; coldly*) George, if you can control the animal in you for just one minute . . . !

GEORGE (*holding the dress close to himself, lovingly*) Go away! Leave me with my wicked thoughts! (*Holding the dress out again; irritably*) Why isn't the damn thing filled!

BASIL (*moving* L *of George; impatiently*) George—sympathetic as I am with the—er—Winter of your discontent . . .

GEORGE (*almost in a trance; looking at him*) H'mmm?

BASIL. Put the damn thing down! (*He snatches the dress from George and throws it on the settee*)

GEORGE (*with shrug of shoulders*) I suppose you're being cruel only to be kind. (*Indicating the silver*) Where does this lot go?

BASIL. You'd better ask Barbara.

GEORGE (*with a doubtful look towards the kitchen*) 'Mmm!

BASIL. Or perhaps *I* had.

GEORGE. D'you think perhaps if we presented a united front . . . ?

(DELIA *comes from the kitchen carrying the ironing-board.* BARBARA *follows with the iron*)

(*Rising; chirpily*) Hello, girls! (*Rushing to Delia and taking board from her*) Here! Let me! Where do you want it?

BARBARA (*giving George the iron as well, and pointing* L) Over there by the plug.

(GEORGE, *as unobtrusively as possible, plugs in the iron and stands it flat on the floor, then attempts to put ironing-board up.* DELIA *moves above the settee*)

BASIL. George has made a fine job of the silver, don't you think, Babs?

BARBARA (*moving* R *of the settee and looking at it*) Which has he done?

GEORGE. What? Why all of it! (*He is having trouble with ironing-board*)

BARBARA. You don't say! Oh, yes! I can see now—just.

BASIL (*sitting* L *on the settee and picking up a vase*) Nice to see the family plate out again. We ought to use it more often, Babs. Remember this? It was a wedding present from my Aunt Lucy.

(DELIA *scrutinizes Faith Brantingham's dress almost viciously*)

BARBARA. I remember. I also remember what she said when she gave it to me.

BASIL. What did she say?

BARBARA. "I *hope* you'll be happy, but you don't know what you're letting yourself in for." (*Looking quickly towards George and Delia*) How right she was!

(GEORGE, *who has been having high jinks with the ironing-board, trying to set it up, suddenly lets it collapse and gives a yell of agony and dances around, shaking his hand and sucking his thumb alternately*)

GEORGE. *Ow!*

DELIA (*turning to George*) Now what's the matter?

GEORGE. My thumb! That lousy thing! (*Kicking the collapsed ironing-board*) Ow! of all the damn-fool contraptions!

BARBARA (*indignantly*) George, do you *mind*?

GEORGE (*dancing around*) Of course I mind. (*Nursing his hand*) I shan't be able to use this hand for weeks.

DELIA. Thank God for that!

BARBARA. Delia, will you please get the ironing-board up and this dress ironed and out of the way.

(DELIA, *muttering, gets the dress from the settee and moves up to the board. During the next dialogue she too has difficulty with the board*)

You men! Ask you to do one small job and you make a dozen.

GEORGE (*moving to the french windows*) I don't mind doing a man's job, but juggling with ruddy ironing-boards . . . ! (*Irritably*) Why doesn't the woman have her dresses made of that "drip-dry" stuff! (*Looking at his finger*) I say, this finger's going blue!

BASIL. They always do before they drop off. Why worry?

(DELIA *gives a yell of agony, sucks a finger and gives the collapsed board a vicious kick*)

DELIA (*yelling, and dancing round*) Ow!

BARBARA (*beginning to lose patience again*) For heaven's sake . . . !

BASIL (*rising*) Delia, have you hurt yourself? (*He rushes to her*)

BARBARA. Well, really, Delia, if you don't know how to put up an ironing-board—at your age!

BASIL (*unthinkingly*) Now, now, Babs! Don't be catty! (*He unconsciously takes Delia's hand in his*)

BARBARA (*stunned*) Catty! Basil Martin, did you say . . . ?

DELIA (*taking her hand out of Basil's, sucking her finger, and wagging her hand alternately*) There's something wrong with the damn thing. (*Turning on George*) It's your fault! Kicking it the way you did! (*To Basil, who takes her hand unconsciously*) Thank you, Basil.

BARBARA. Basil, I demand an apology!

GEORGE (*to Delia*) Do you know how to put up an ironing-board, or don't you? (*His finger is still giving pain*)

BARBARA. Basil Martin . . .

DELIA (*shouting at George*) No, I *don't*. (*Again to Basil*) Thank you, Basil.

BASIL (*clasping his head*) Barbara, darling, *please* . . .

GEORGE (*shouting to Delia*) Then you won't marry me till you ruddy well *do*!

BARBARA (*suddenly shouting at George*) George, will you kindly stop shouting in my house?

DELIA (*moving* L *of George*) I wouldn't marry you if . . .

BASIL (*moving to* L *of Barbara*) For God's sake, Babs, stop shouting like that!

BARBARA (*at the top of her voice*) I'll shout as much as I like!

(BARBARA *crosses* BASIL *and puts up the ironing-board*)

DELIA. Well, really . . . !

GEORGE (*furiously to Delia*) And what are you "well really-ing" about?

DELIA (*furiously*) Don't you talk to me!

GEORGE. I don't want to talk to you. I wouldn't demean myself to talk to a woman who couldn't put up a ruddy ironing-board!

BASIL. George! How dare you speak to Delia like that?

BARBARA. Before I go stark raving mad . . . ! Delia! Will you please get that woman's dress ironed, and Basil, will you take George out into the garden and let him do his bellowing in the green-house!

BASIL (*moving up to her at ironing-board; firmly*) Now listen, Barbara, heaven knows I am a patient man . . . !

BARBARA. And heaven knows you'll *need to be* for the rest of your married life!

BASIL. I've put up with a great deal this morning!

DELIA (*whimpering*) I want to go home to mother!

BARBARA (*to Basil; unbelievingly*) *You* . . . have . . . put . . . up with a great deal!

BASIL. I have indeed!

BARBARA. You *dare* say that to me!

DELIA (*whimpering again*) I want to go home . . .

GEORGE (*moving to below the settee*) Then why the hell don't you?

(DELIA *follows to* L *of George*)

BASIL (*pleadingly*) Barbara . . .

DELIA (*shouting at George*) Because I haven't got the fare! (*She crosses George to down* R)

BARBARA (*repeating slowly and furiously*) You have put up with a great deal . . . !

BASIL (*snapping, in a raised voice*) Do you *have* to keep harping on like that? I should have thought the fact was obvious! From the first moment I came downstairs this morning I—I—(*searching for words*)—*I have put up with a great deal*!

GEORGE (*placatingly, to Basil*) Steady as she goes, old boy!

BASIL (*turning on him, snapping*) Go to hell! (*He moves up to the desk*)

GEORGE (*unbelievingly*) Did you hear that? Basil—my old pal—telling me to go to hell!

DELIA. I don't care where you go so long as you don't come to London!

BASIL (*moving* L *of George; wildly*) George, old man, I apologize. I—I—didn't mean—but with Babs nagging at me . . . !

BARBARA (*indignantly*) Nagging!

BASIL (*to her; sharply*) Nagging! Nag, nag, nag! And just because there's a little lunch to prepare! No thought, of course, for what that little lunch might lead to!

BARBARA. You call roast chicken and all the etceteras that go with it a *little* lunch? Here am I, on the hottest day in September, slaving over a hot stove . . . !

BASIL. But, good God, woman, can't you see further than the end of your nose? Are you my wife, or aren't you?

BARBARA. I *am*, I *am*! (*Wailing*) Oh! Why didn't I listen to your Aunt Lucy!

GEORGE. Now—Basil—Barbara . . .

BASIL. I don't understand you. I just *don't* understand you, Barbara! Here's George—who is not my wife—(*quickly appealing to George*)—are you?

GEORGE (*shaking his head solemnly*) No, old man.

BASIL (*sweeping on, to Barbara*) Here's George, who is not my wife; who stands to gain nothing; goes to all the trouble he has—at risk of life and limb to get Faith Brantingham up here, purely for *my* sake . . .

DELIA (*viciously*) I wouldn't be too sure of that!

GEORGE (*quickly*) Shut up! (*To Basil*) Go on, old man!

BASIL. Where was I?

GEORGE. I, who am not your wife, who stand to gain nothing, go to all the trouble at risk of life and limb . . .

Basil (*irritably*) All right! All right! (*To Barbara*) Well, surely—surely—if George can do that in—in friendship's name . . .

Barbara (*almost gibbering*) Of all the mawkish drivel . . . !

Basil (*carried away*) . . . then surely you, my wife . . . (*Suddenly*) Did you say "drivel"?

Barbara. *Mawkish* drivel! And if the dialogue in your play is half as mawkish—then a ten course banquet at the Savoy, given to every actress in London, wouldn't get it produced!

Basil (*furiously*) Right! That settles it! I'm finished! Through! George!

George. Yes, old boy?

Basil. Go upstairs, get Faith Brantingham, take her out of this house and put her back where you found her!

George. What . . . ?

Basil (*grandly*) Just that!

George. But, Bas . . .

Basil. Since my wife has such a low opinion of my—my humble talents . . .

Barbara. It isn't *low*—it's non-existent!

Basil (*turning to her*) Barbara!

Barbara (*acidly to Delia*) Delia, are you going to iron this dress or are you not?

Basil. Not until you have apologized for . . .

Barbara. I am talking to Delia!

Basil. Damn Delia!

Delia (*squeaking*) Basil!

Basil. I mean damn the dress! Barbara, are you going to apologize?

Barbara. Most certainly not!

Basil. I shall count three!

Barbara. You can count . . .

Basil. And if, in that time, you haven't apologized for all the insults you've hurled at me, *in public*, I walk out of this house for ever!

Barbara. Is that a promise?

George. Now, look, old boy, I'm sure . . .

Basil. One!

Delia (*to George*) You keep out of this! (*Pushing George away and crossing to Basil*) It's nothing to do with you! Basil, when you go, can I come with you?

Basil. *Two!* What did you say, Delia?

George (*pushing Delia down* R *and crossing her to Basil*) Nothing. She never does! (*Pleading*) Bas, old boy.

Barbara (*crossing Basil to* L *of George; threateningly*) George, if you persuade him to change his mind . . .

Basil (*in ringing voice*) Three! (*He raises an arm*) Barbara, goodbye! This is the end! (*He brings the flat of his hand down on to the ironing-board very forcefully. It collapses. At once his old self*) Oh, my God!

(*They all look at the ironing-board*)

GEORGE. Blimey!

BASIL. Babs—darling—I—I . . . (*He picks up the ironing-board and tries to put it up*)

BARBARA (*her voice trembling with emotion*) Go away! All of you—please—go away.

BASIL (*as the ironing-board collapses to floor again; loudly, wildly*) What's the *matter* with the *damn* thing?

BARBARA (*clutching her head with both hands*) Leave it! Leave it! (*She crosses below George and sits on the settee*)

BASIL. But—darling . . .

BARBARA (*drumming her hands on her knees*) Basil . . . !

BASIL (*moving towards her eagerly*) Yes, dear? (*He trips over the ironing-board*) Aaah!

GEORGE (*moving to Basil; stoically*) Steady as she goes, old boy.

(BASIL *kneels* L *of Barbara*)

BARBARA. Will you please—take yourself, George and Delia out of here?

BASIL. But—but—where can we go?

BARBARA (*in a just controlled voice*) There must be somewhere! It's a very large world!

BASIL. But . . .

BARBARA. Take them into the garden. Show them the hollyhocks.

BASIL. George has seen 'em.

BARBARA (*at screaming point*) Delia hasn't.

GEORGE (*moving to the fireplace; muttering*) She wouldn't know a hollyhock from a caterpillar!

BASIL (*rising; wretchedly*) Delia, come into the garden and see the . . .

DELIA. But—Barbara—this mess! Can't I help?

BARBARA (*rising and running round* R *of the settee, shooing Delia and Basil into the garden; wildly*) Yes, you can! By going into the garden and seeing the caterpillars—hollyhocks!

(BASIL *and* DELIA *exit through the french windows, chased by* BARBARA. GEORGE *picks up the ironing-board*)

GEORGE. I'm damned if I'll be beaten! (*He tries to fix the ironing-board*)

BARBARA (*moving down to George; angrily*) George . . . !

GEORGE (*fiddling with board*) O.K. Barbara. (*Puzzled*) I suppose there's a knack.

BARBARA (*snatching the board from him*) It's as simple as this. (*She puts the board up quickly*) Now, will you, *please* . . .

GEORGE (*gaping at the board*) Good Lord! Fancy! (*He puts his hands on it to test it. It collapses again*)

(BARBARA *gives a despairing cry*)

(*Muttering*) Fancy!

(GEORGE *dashes off into garden after others.* BARBARA, *alone gives a whimper, picks up the board, turns it over, looks at it despairingly, lets it collapse to the floor, moves away. She again whimpers. She picks up the dress, looks at it despairingly, then begins to sob. Unconsciously she dabs her eyes with the dress, then realizing what she is doing, gives a loud moan, throws the dress on to settee and, sobbing loudly, totters through the kitchen door leaving it slightly ajar. As* BARBARA *enters the kitchen, the* MILKMAN *is heard rattling milk bottles as in Act One. He enters through the back door carrying a bottle in each hand. Seeing Barbara in tears he, almost mechanically, opens his arms*)

MILKMAN (*not surprised, but sympathetically*) Mrs—Martin!

BARBARA (*as she totters towards him*) Oh—Milkman! (*And she is in his arms*)

MILKMAN (*arms round her, but still holding the bottles*) There—there, Mrs Martin.

BARBARA (*her head on his chest, sobbing*) Oh, milkman!

MILKMAN. There—there . . . ! (*He realizes he is still holding the bottles. With his arms around Barbara, he edges her nearer the table so that he can put the bottles down. Having done so, gingerly, he holds her closer and begins to sway*) There—there, Mrs Martin! (*After they have swayed for a time—his face on her hair—trying to speak practically*) I've brought the milk, Mrs Martin.

BARBARA (*gulping*) Th-hank you, milkman. (*They are still swaying*)

MILKMAN. Two pints!

BARBARA. Thank you.

(*They sway for a little*)

MILKMAN (*after kissing her hair*) That'll be one and sixpence extra.

BARBARA (*in between sobs, snuggling up to him*) Yes, it will, won't it?

MILKMAN (*also snuggling up*) Yes, ma'am.

(*They sway for a while in silence, except for an occasional sob from* BARBARA)

Making this week's bill nine and a penny altogether.

BARBARA (*drawing away ever so slightly so that she can look up into his face, puzzled, but not querulous*) Nine and . . . ?

MILKMAN (*still holding her; quietly*) There was that two shillings worth of cream you had last Sunday, ma'am—remember?

BARBARA (*softly*) I remember. (*She snuggles up again. After a slight pause; with a little sob*) I'd better get it. (*She makes as if to move out of his arms*)

MILKMAN. What ma'am?

BARBARA. The nine and a penny.

MILKMAN (*drawing her close again*) No hurry, ma'am! (*He now strokes her hair. They sway. After a long silence*) Lovely weather, isn't it?

BARBARA (*agreeing, and gulping*) Mmmmps!

MILKMAN (*still swaying*) Hasn't been a bad summer on the whole.
BARBARA. No.

(*A pause, while they sway*)

MILKMAN (*softly*) My half-day this afternoon.
BARBARA. Oh!
MILKMAN. Yes. I'm going out into the country.
BARBARA. Are you?
MILKMAN. We have visitors at home; drive me up the wall. I want to get away from 'em.
BARBARA. I'm sure you do. (*A pause. With a gulp*) Where are you going?
MILKMAN. Oh—up on the Downs somewhere for a couple of hours—where it's quiet and peaceful.
BARBARA (*with a sob and a sigh*) Wonderful!
MILKMAN (*after a pause*) Going on my Scooter.
BARBARA. Scooter?
MILKMAN. Motor scooter.
BARBARA (*sighing*) Heaven!

(*There is quite a longish pause*)

MILKMAN. There's room for two, ma'am.
BARBARA (*slightly startled*) You mean . . . ?
MILKMAN. On the Scooter.
BARBARA. But . . .
MILKMAN (*softly*) It's up to you, ma'am.
BARBARA (*murmuring, doubtfully*) Thank you—but . . .
MILKMAN (*swaying*) Nice to get away from your—*troubles*—once in a while.
BARBARA (*after a slight pause*) What time are you . . . ?
MILKMAN (*softly*) About three o'clock.
BARBARA. Oh!
MILKMAN. Got to wash and change and have my dinner first.
BARBARA. Yes, of course.
MILKMAN (*rubbing his face gently on her hair*) And I don't finish till one.
BARBARA (*after a slight pause*) Will you be—passing this way?
MILKMAN (*after a slight pause*) If I forgot to take the nine and a penny *now* I could—er . . .
BARBARA (*after a slight pause*) I wonder if *I* could . . .
MILKMAN (*after a slight pause*) Lovely up on the Downs, ma'am . . .
BARBARA (*after a gulp*) I'll try!

(*They snuggle up closer.* DELIA *and* GEORGE *enter through the french windows. In the kitchen,* BARBARA *and the* MILKMAN *draw apart the moment* DELIA *speaks*)

DELIA (*moving* L *of the settee; fairly loudly*) If I hear another word about hollyhocks I'll . . . (*She stops speaking abruptly and begins sniffing*)

(BARBARA *moves quietly to the connecting door and closes it, then returns to near the Milkman*)

GEORGE (*fairly loudly, almost at the same time as Delia*) Now listen to me, my girl. It's about time you . . . (*He too stops speaking and sniffs*)

MILKMAN (*after a look toward the living-room; quietly*) Three o'clock?

(DELIA *moves* R *of the settee, sniffing*)

BARBARA (*smiling at him*) I'll try.

(GEORGE *moves* L *of the settee, sniffing*)

MILKMAN. Try very hard, ma'am.

(*The* MILKMAN *backs to the kitchen door, smiling at Barbara, and exits.* BARBARA *looks after him, almost in a trance. Then, all trace of anguish gone, she moves to the mirror down* R *and, during the following dialogue, pats her hair, looks at her reflection happily and, humming "Plaisir d'Amour" quietly, twirls around the room*)

DELIA (*rather alarmed*) George—something's burning!

GEORGE. You're right, ducks! I thought I could smell . . . and it's in *here* too!

(BASIL *comes in through the french windows*)

BASIL (*moving down* L; *nervously*) George, Delia, don't you think you ought to . . . (*With a yelp*) My God! Something's burning!

DELIA (*alarmed*) I know. I was just saying to George . . .

(*They all dart about trying to locate the trouble.* BASIL *takes the ironing-board upstage to the armchair*)

BASIL (*almost demented at once*) What is it? Oh, my Lord, what is it? If Barbara . . . !

DELIA (*crossing below the settee to* L; *with a yell*) The iron!

GEORGE. What?

DELIA (*pointing to it*) Look! It's on! (*She rushes to wall and unplugs it*)

BASIL (*at the same time*) No!

(*They gather round the iron,* BASIL R *of Delia,* GEORGE R *of Basil*)

BASIL. Oh, my heavens—the carpet! It *hasn't* . . . ?

DELIA (*wildly*) I daren't look! I daren't look! (*She covers her eyes with her hands, then turns on George*) George, did *you* plug it in?

GEORGE (*babbling*) I—I . . .

DELIA (*crossing below Basil to George and beating his chest with her clenched hands*) You did! You did! (*Turning to Basil, whimpering*) Oh Basil . . . !

(BASIL *slowly bends down and lifts the iron. On the carpet is an iron-shaped patch of dark brown*)

BASIL (*in anguish, as he sees it*) Aaaah!

(DELIA *gives a howl*)

GEORGE. Blimey? (*He kneels*)

(DELIA *kneels*)

BASIL (*babbling*) George—fetch a razor—cut my throat—anything rather than . . . (*he looks towards the kitchen*)

(*They all concentrate on the burnt carpet.* BASIL *rubs at it frantically.* BARBARA, *with a radiant smile on her face, passes through the connecting door into the living-room*)

BARBARA (*in the doorway; gaily*) Hello, there!

(*The three on the floor start guiltily, and give little yelps*)

(*With genuine amusement*) What on earth are you all doing down on your knees like that? (*She moves down* R *of the settee*)

(*They all begin talking at once*)

BASIL		Babs—darling—with my hand on my heart . . . !
GEORGE	(*together*)	Look, Barbara, old girl—it was an accident. You see, I thought . . .
DELIA		(*near to hysteria*) Blame George, Barbara. It wasn't me. I never went near the thing.

BARBARA (*moving to the* L *end of the settee; quite happily*) What are you all jabbering about?

(BASIL *again prostrates himself Moslem fashion*)

DELIA (*wildly*) The carpet!

BARBARA (*curiously, but calmly*) The carpet?

GEORGE (*babbling*) Barbara, I don't know how to apologize . . .

BARBARA. For *what*, for heaven's sake?

DELIA (*still wildly*) The *carpet*! It's burnt . . . ! The iron—George plugged it in and left it on! (*She reveals the burn*) Look!

BASIL (*in anguish*) Aaaah!

BARBARA (*looking at the burn; not unduly disturbed*) Oh, dear! (*Then, quite pleasantly and brightly*) Never mind—George!

BASIL (*it is almost a squawk*) What did you say?

BARBARA. Never mind! Worse things happen at sea! (*And, with her thoughts elsewhere, she begins to hum "Plasir d'Amour" and twirls above the settee and into the kitchen, completely lost to everything except her extreme happiness*)

The three on the floor gape at her open-mouthed as—

the CURTAIN *falls*

ACT III

SCENE—*The same. 12.40 p.m., the same day.*

The room has been tidied, and the burnt part of the carpet covered with a rug. The coffee-table has been removed and the furniture opened out so that the table from up C can be brought to LC. It is now in position, with its leaves open. It has been laid for lunch, and looks very attractive. Five places are laid. Drinks have also been set out on their shelves.

When the CURTAIN *rises,* BASIL *is standing uneasily by the french windows and* GEORGE *is sitting on the settee, a copy of Basil's play on his lap. Actually, he is almost dropping off to sleep. His head nods once or twice.*

BASIL (*as he moves down* L) What's the time?

(*No answer from George*)

(*Louder*) George!

GEORGE (*looking up, startled*) Eh? What's that, old man?

BASIL (*slightly irritably*) What's the time?

GEORGE (*after a big yawn*) Dammit, I told you five minutes ago. (*Consulting his watch*) Twenty to one.

BASIL (*moving to the table*) My watch has stopped.

GEORGE. Might not be a bad idea to wind it up.

(BASIL, *moves up to the hall, looks up the stairs, then comes restlessly back into the room, to* R *of the settee*)

BASIL (*muttering*) Why doesn't she come down?

GEORGE (*vaguely, as he reads*) Who? Faith Brantingham?

BASIL (*snapping*) No. Babs.

GEORGE. Good God! What do you want *her* to come down for?

BASIL (*frigidly*) I beg your pardon?

GEORGE. "Let sleeping dogs lie."

BASIL (*indignantly*) George!

GEORGE (*realizing he has said the wrong thing*) I mean—I—I—well—er—you know what I meant, Bas, old boy.

BASIL (*still frigidly*) No, I don't!

GEORGE (*non-plussed*) Oh! Well, er . . . (*Suddenly and heartily, looking towards the hall*) Ah! *Here* she is!

BASIL (*his old nervous self*) What? (*Spinning round to face the hall; babbling*) Babs—darling—I—I . . . (*He stops when he sees there is no one there. He turns, facing George*)

GEORGE (*smiling*) *That's* what I meant!

BASIL (*furiously*) George! (*He moves above the settee*) That was not funny.

GEORGE (*muttering*) Bloody tragic—if you ask me!

BASIL (*looking on the shelves up* C) Wish to the Lord I could find my pipe. Might feel better for a smoke. Oh, hell!

(BASIL *crosses to the table and nervously moves the things about on it*)

GEORGE (*seeing this*) Now, now!

BASIL. What?

GEORGE. I've told you before—don't muck about with the table. It's fine as it is. And you don't want Barbara to . . . Why don't you come and sit down.

BASIL (*coming to the settee and sitting by George*) I'm too het up to sit down. (*Wretchedly*) Oh, Lord!

GEORGE. Now what? Look, old man, I'm trying to read this play of yours. I'd better have *some* idea of what it's about when we—er—get to work on "Madam".

BASIL. How far have you got?

GEORGE. Page—(*he looks at the script*)—Two.

BASIL (*rising and moving away to the fireplace; heavily*) You're doing fine! Only another hundred and eighteen to get through.

GEORGE (*rather dolefully*) H'm! I haven't come to any funny bits yet.

BASIL (*dolefully*) If you *do*, for heaven's sake let me know.

GEORGE (*puzzled*) What?

BASIL. There aren't supposed to *be* any! (*After a restless movement*) You know, George, old boy, I'm not sure that we haven't gone to all this trouble for nothing.

GEORGE. You mean the woman won't read the play?

BASIL. She may read it, but—I'm sure she'll never play the part. I realize that more than ever now I've actually seen her—all of her, and there's a hell of a lot of her, isn't there? (*He indicates the bust*) And dash it all—the part—well, she's a nun.

GEORGE. What of it?

BASIL. Well—(*indicating the bust again*)—I mean to say . . . !

GEORGE (*almost impatiently*) But good Lord, nuns have them, don't they? I know they get rid of their *hair*, but surely they don't get rid of . . .

BASIL (*frigidly*) George, please!

(DELIA *comes downstairs and into the living-room, carrying a tray with a glass and a "tonic" bottle on it*)

(*Seeing her*) My Heavens! Not *another*?

DELIA (*shortly*) No! She's in the bathroom. I whipped into the bedroom and grabbed the tray—I thought that perhaps . . .

BASIL (*moving up towards the stairs*) "Out of sight—out of mind!" Good for you, Delia. ((*With a nervous look towards the stairs*) You say she's in the bathroom?

DELIA. She is. (*She moves towards the kitchen door*)

BASIL (*nervously, looking towards the hall*) Then . . .

GEORGE. What's she doing in there?

DELIA (*snapping at him*) Would you like me to look through the keyhole and find out?

GEORGE (*with indignation*) Certainly not! (*Half rising; with interest*) Is there a keyhole?

BASIL. George! ! ! (*rather pompously*) *Nemo allegans suam turpitudinem audiendus*

(*The translation of which is:* "*No one testifying to his own baseness should be listened to*")

DELIA (*witheringly*) And what does *that* mean?

GEORGE (*grinning*) "Bags I the first peep!"

BASIL. George, please! ! (*to Delia*) And where's Barbara?

DELIA. In her bedroom . . . singing!

BASIL. *Still* singing?

DELIA. Huh-huh!

BASIL (*troubled*) I wonder if I *ought* to get the doctor! (*He moves to the desk*)

GEORGE. Why should you?

BASIL. I don't like it.

GEORGE. Barbara's singing?

BASIL (*frigidly*) The fact that she *is* singing. I mean to say—what's she got to sing about?

GEORGE. P'raps she's happy.

BASIL. Don't talk nonsense! How *could* she be?

DELIA (*somewhat apprehensively*) Do you mean she never is?

BASIL (*testily*) Of course she *is*—often—in so far as married life permits, but . . .

DELIA (*more apprehensive*) *What?*

BASIL (*moving L of the table*) She certainly wasn't happy about this lunch for Faith Brantingham and that's still *on*—so I just don't understand . . .

(BARBARA *comes downstairs and into room. She has changed into a pretty dress and is still cheerful*)

BARBARA (*brightly*) Hello, what are you all up to?

(GEORGE *immediately leaps up from settee to* R *of it.* DELIA *and* BASIL *almost spring to attention*)

BASIL (*nervously*) Nothing—nothing—I was just . . . (*He crosses to Delia and takes the tray from her*) Shall I take that, Delia? I'll wash the glass . . .

DELIA (*trying to hang on to the tray*) No, no, I'll take it. (*With a nervous look towards Barbara*) I'll wash it.

BARBARA. You'll neither of you wash it. (*Taking the tray from Delia*) I will. Sit down, Delia, you look worn out. Basil!

(DELIA *moves to the armchair and sits*)

BASIL. Yes, dear?

BARBARA. Get poor Delia a drink, darling.

(*They all react to the affectionate "darling"*)

What would you like, Delia?

DELIA (*muttering*) Oh—er—anything . . .

BARBARA. Did you say "anything" or "everything"?

DELIA. I—I . . .

BARBARA. You can have either.

DELIA (*muttering*) I'd like a tomato juice.

GEORGE (*to Delia*) You sickening for something?

DELIA (*snapping*) I can have a tomato juice if I want one, can't I?

BARBARA. 'Fraid not, Delia. We haven't got one. (*She takes the tray into the kitchen*)

(DELIA *whimpers exasperatedly*)

BASIL (*nervously*) Shall I slip out and get some?

(BARBARA *puts the tray on the kitchen table*)

GEORGE (*cheerfully*) Good God, no. It isn't worth it. (*He sits R on the settee*)

DELIA (*beginning to weep*) You see! That's how much he thinks of me.

BASIL (*moving towards her consolingly*) Delia . . .

(BARBARA *comes from the kitchen.* BASIL *sits R on the settee*)

DELIA. I'm not even worth a tomato juice!

BARBARA (*moving R of the armchair; brightly*) Now, now, come along, Delia, pull yourself together. Miss Brantingham will be down any minute and we must all be bright and cheerful.

DELIA. Why should I be bright and cheerful? I've done nothing but run after the woman from the first moment she got here. Nobody else has.

BARBARA (*a little snappily*) Of course, if you think I've been slaving over a hot stove all the morning just for fun . . . !

BASIL (*rising quickly*) Is everything ready, Babs? (*He moves L of Barbara*)

BARBARA. It is.

GEORGE. Good for you, Barbara. Now look, we ought to have a plan of campaign.

BASIL (*nervously*) How do you mean?

GEORGE. Well—regarding this play of Basil's—we've got to be tactful in the way we mention it, haven't we? We've got to choose the right moment, so to speak.

BARBARA (*crossing below the armchair to L of it*) All I beg is that you don't choose any moment during lunch. Let's get that ordeal over first.

BASIL. Ordeal?

BARBARA (*to Basil*) We don't entertain ginned-up celebrities every day, do we? What I suggest is that you and George choose a moment *after* lunch. I'll bring your coffee in and retire gracefully into the kitchen. I'm sure Miss Brantingham would prefer that as much as I would.

DELIA. And what do I do while all this is going on?

BARBARA. Help me wash up.

GEORGE (*heartily*) Damn good idea. We'll handle her better on our own, won't we, Bas, old boy?

BARBARA. How long do you think it's going to take?

GEORGE (*with a smirk*) Depends how far we have to go!

DELIA (*whimpering*) Oooh!

BARBARA (*crossing below Delia and Basil to* L *of the settee*) Well, while you're going—as far as you have to I'm going out!

BASIL. Out? Out where?

BARBARA (*brightly*) Up on the Downs. (*She begins to twirl happily*).

BASIL (*gaping at her*) Up on the . . . ?

BARBARA. Why not? After a somewhat trying morning, I feel a little air . . . Besides—as George has so tactfully pointed out— you and he may have to—er—go *far* with Miss Brantingham. Well, darling, I'm sure it would be a much more comfortable journey if you knew I was out of the way. (*She twists*).

BASIL (*shocked*) But, good heavens, Barbara, you don't imagine for one moment that—I don't know what George has in mind!

DELIA (*shortly*) I do! The rat!

BARBARA. Yes—well of course, Delia, you know George better than *I* do, but if he intends going as far as you seem to imply, I trust Basil will have the good grace to—er—fall by the wayside!

(*There is a ring at the front door bell*)

BASIL (*starting*) Oh, my . . . ! Who can that be?

BARBARA (*crossing below Basil to the fireplace*) There's a very simple way of finding out.

BASIL. What? Oh, yes. I'll go. But Babs—this—this going up on the Downs—I don't understand it. You never go up on the Downs.

BARBARA. I'll try anything once, darling. (*She twirls*)

BASIL. But . . .

(*The door bell rings again*)

BASIL. Oh, hell!

(BASIL *goes out into hall and off to front door*)

GEORGE (*to Delia*) Do *you* good to get up on the Downs, Delia, old girl.

BARBARA (*startled*) What?

GEORGE (*still at Delia*) Nothing like walking for improving the figure, eh, Barbara?

DELIA. So my figure's all wrong now, is it?

GEORGE. Oh, I daresay it's always been the way it is, but . . .

DELIA (*furiously*) George Padstow!

GEORGE. But that's no reason why you should lose heart. A good long tramp over the Downs with Barbara . . . Eh, Barbara?

BARBARA. No, George.

GEORGE. Eh?

BARBARA. I think it would be better if Delia—stayed here.

GEORGE. Oh—but . . .

BARBARA. After all she *is* engaged to you.

DELIA. You'd never think it—the way he treats me.

BARBARA. All men don't show their affection the same way. (*After a slight pause; smiling*) Indeed they don't! (*She twirls*) But as I was saying—seeing that you're engaged to George—it might be as well if you hang around this afternoon. Er—sit in the garden and look at the hollyhocks. Of *course*, I'm sure you can have the same implicit faith in George that I can in Basil—but to leave him entirely at the mercy of Faith Brantingham . . .

GEORGE (*murmuring ecstatically*) Oh, boy!

BARBARA (*to Delia, after a look at George*) See what I mean.

(BASIL *returns with a bunch of roses*)

(*Seeing the roses*) And what have we here?

BASIL. Roses. (*He moves above* L *of the settee*)

BARBARA. So we have—for Miss Brantingham I presume?

BASIL. Er—yes.

BARBARA. So whatever has to be said to her, is to be said with flowers! And whose idea was that?

DELIA. I'll have one guess. (*Glaring at George*) The rat's!

BASIL (*moving to above* L *of the table*) But, Barbara, they're not from me—or George . . . (*Taking a card from the roses and holding it out to her*) Look, they're from . . .

(BARBARA *takes card and looks at it*)

BARBARA (*reading*) "Your ever adoring Tony". H'mm! It's a long time since *my ever adoring Basil* said anything to me—with flowers.

BASIL. Darling—wait till the play is . . .

DELIA (*to George; witheringly*) Yes! That'll be the day—when *my ever adoring George* comes to *me* with a bunch of flowers in hand!

GEORGE (*grinning*) I'll say it will!

DELIA (*to others*) All I ever see are gins and tonics.

GEORGE (*still grinning*) Well, duckie, why grumble at *that*?

DELIA (*snapping*) Because I've usually paid for them!

BARBARA (*moving to the table*) How do you think the table looks?

BASIL (*moving to her side*) Beautiful, Babs, darling. A work of art. Don't you think so, George?

GEORGE (*rising to* R *of the table*) Smashing when we put the roses in the middle.

BARBARA. Roses. (*Looking at the bunch*) You mean . . . ?
GEORGE (*taking the roses from Basil*) 'Course I do!
BARBARA (*gaping at him*) But those are Miss Brantingham's.
GEORGE (*grinning*) What you've never had you never miss.
BARBARA. But they're from her ever adoring Tony.
BASIL (*nervously*) I must say, George, it seems a bit thick. It's—
er—pinching them, isn't it?
GEORGE. Good Lord, no. (*Moving up* R *of Delia*) She can take
'em with her when she goes! Get me the vase, Delia.
DELIA (*snapping*) Why can't you . . . ?
GEORGE. And shove some water in it.
DELIA. "Do this; do that!"
BASIL. I'll get it! Where is it?
BARBARA (*with just a touch of the old Babs*) Oh . . . ! Sit down all
of you. I'll get it.
DELIA (*rising*) Certainly not, Barbara. Mr Padstow has ordered
me to get it and get it I must.
GEORGE (*snapping at her*) Well, get it and stop yapping about
it!
DELIA. Yapping?
GEORGE (*desperately*) Blind O'Reilly! (*He looks around, sees the
silver vase on the shelves* C *and gets it*) I'll get it myself. Hold these (*He
hands the roses to Delia and moves towards kitchen*)
BARBARA (*taking a step after him; anxiously*) Go carefully in that
kitchen, George; we don't want any disasters in there.

GEORGE (*continuing on his way, still muttering*) Ask a
woman to do one small job and there's as
much fuss as if you'd let her pants down
(*together*) and given her a damn good hiding. (*He goes
to the sink*)
DELIA (*following him, roses in hand*) Give it to me!
You told me to get it, and there'd have
been no fuss if you'd asked me decently.

(*Solo*) The trouble is, George Padstow, you're taking things too much
for granted. (*She stands close behind him*)
GEORGE (*at the tap, running water in*) I'm beginning to wonder if I
shouldn't have done that sooner—when you fell in the river at
Richmond; taken it for granted and left you there.

(*In the meantime, BARBARA, in the living-room, is talking to Basil*)

BARBARA (*the moment George goes into the kitchen*) I wish George
wouldn't interfere. The table looks perfectly all right as it is,
doesn't it?
BASIL. Lovely, darling—wonderful—superb . . .
BARBARA (*snapping a little*) That's enough! (*She moves to the mantelpiece*) Don't overdo it! Then why clutter it up with flowers? And I
shouldn't be surprised if they're not covered with green-fly!
BASIL (*moving up* C) I'll tell him we don't want them.

(GEORGE, *with* DELIA *at heel, comes into the living-room and moves below the settee to above the table*)

DELIA (*replying to George's last remark*) Of all the wicked things to say! (*Whimpering*) Barbara, what do you think George has just said?
BARBARA. I daren't *begin* to think.
BASIL (*moving down* C, R *of Delia*) George—old man . . .
DELIA. He says he ought to have left me there when I fell in the river at Richmond.
BARBARA. Anyone can be wise *after* the event

(DELIA *reacts to this*)

BASIL. George—old man, do we really need the flowers? I don't see that a few roses are going to make much difference one way or the other.
DELIA (*tetchily*) Let him have his way, Basil, for goodness sake, or we'll all have to suffer for it. Here! Take your roses.

(DELIA *thrusts the roses at* GEORGE, *who is standing, vase in hand, over the table*)

BASIL. But is there room for them? George . . .
GEORGE (*exasperatedly*) Of course there's room! Look! (*He jabs the roses into the vase almost viciously. As the vase is full to the brim with water, water spurts all over the table*)

(*Shouts of alarm and horror from all*)

BARBARA (*wildly*) George!
BASIL (*with a howl*) George—oh, George!
DELIA (*running down* R) You idiot! Now look what you've . . .
GEORGE. I—I . . . (*He is so shaken that he jabs the roses further into the vase, causing more water to spurt over the table*)

(*More shouts from all*)

Oh, Lord! (*Now in a complete dither he drops vase on table*)
BASIL (*flinging himself on the settee, face downwards and beating a cushion with clenched fists*) Aaaah!
DELIA (*menacingly; rushing towards George*) You . . . you . . .
BARBARA (*moving above to between George and Delia*) Delia!
DELIA. Let me get at him! Let me get at him!
GEORGE (*tremulously*) Steady as she goes, old girl!
DELIA (*livid*) Oooh! (*She rushes to the settee to fling herself on it. Finding Basil already there*) Make room for me! (*She unceremoniously gives Basil a push which sends him on to the floor. She flings herself on the settee and pummels the cushion with both hands*)
GEORGE (*dithering*) I—I—I'll fetch something to wipe it all up.
BARBARA (*seething*) George, if you value your life you won't move an inch!
GEORGE. What? But . . .

BARBARA. Basil! (*Hardly realizing what she is doing, she picks things up from the table and replaces them*)
BASIL (*still on the floor*) Aaaah!
BARBARA. Fetch the large tray from the kitchen, and hurry!
BASIL. Babs—darling . . .
BARBARA (*shouting*) Hurry!
BASIL. Tray—tray . . . (*On hands and knees he crawls towards the kitchen door. It is only when he is at the door that he realizes what he is doing and gets to his feet. He goes through into the kitchen and fetches a large tray from the dresser*)
BARBARA (*meanwhile*) Delia, pull yourself together and give me a hand.
GEORGE (*tremulously*) Can't I . . . ?
BARBARA (*it is almost a scream*) No! Keep away, George. (*She moves L of the settee*) Delia, are you going to help or not?

(GEORGE *moves to the fireplace*)

DELIA (*rising from settee; hysterically*) Send George away, Barbara. Can't you send him away? (*She moves R of the settee*)
BARBARA (*snapping*) He's your property, not mine!

(BASIL *returns with the tray*)

BASIL. The tray, darling. (*He moves R of the table*)
BARBARA (*wailing*) Look! (*Moving above the table*) Water everywhere! Everything will have to come off the table. We shall want fresh mats and . . .
DELIA (*again rushing at George*) Oooh you . . .
BARBARA (*loudly and sharply*) Delia!
DELIA (*stopping C*) I'll kill him!
BARBARA. You will not!
DELIA (*wildly*) I'll do as I like. You just said he was my property.

(BASIL *holds the tray while* BARBARA *puts things from the table on it*)

BARBARA. Basil, take George out of here—again!
GEORGE (*now getting rather huffy*) There's no need for Basil to take me. I can go under my own steam.
DELIA (*moving up R*) Then why don't you?
GEORGE. All right, I will! (*Moving towards the window, then stopping*) But if you don't mind my saying so I take a pretty dim view of the way I'm being treated!
BASIL (*troubled*) What? Now look, George, there's no need to . . .
GEORGE. Whatever I've done, I've done with the best intentions.
BARBARA (*taking sopping linen mat from table and wringing water out of it*) Thanks very much! (*She drops the mat on the tray*)

(BARBARA *goes into the kitchen and gets a swab cloth from the sink*)

BASIL (*conscience-stricken on George's behalf*) Now—Babs—George . . .

GEORGE (*in an injured tone*) No one can help accidents happening now and again. I'm sorry about the table.
DELIA (*moving* R *of George*) And about the bathwater!
GEORGE (*agreeing*) And about the bathwater.
DELIA (*viciously*) And the ironing-board.
GEORGE. And the . . .
DELIA. And the iron! *And* the burnt carpet!
GEORGE. And the iron and the burnt . . .
BASIL (*pleadingly*) Delia, there's no need to . . .
GEORGE. But when Bas's play is put on—thanks to me, and when he's a ruddy millionaire—thanks to me . . .
DELIA. And poor Barbara's in a looney bin—thanks to you . . . !

(BARBARA *returns from the kitchen with the swab cloth and a tea cloth*)

GEORGE (*moving towards her*) Barbara—I . . .
BARBARA (*as she moves towards table; heavily*) Hallo, George! (*As she swabs the table*) What's the time? At the rate we're going we shall be lucky if we get lunch over by midnight.
GEORGE. Barbara, I just want to apologize for—everything.
BARBARA (*grimly*) Bless you!
GEORGE. But I was just telling Delia, no one can help accidents happening now and again.
BARBARA. Nor all the time, seemingly! Basil, put that tray down somewhere while I find fresh mats, if we have any. (*Handing Delia the dry tea cloth*) Delia, wipe the table over with this, will you.

(DELIA *wipes the table.* BASIL *hovers, then puts the tray on the settee and sits.* BARBARA *goes to the kitchen and looks in the dresser, then comes to the door*)

(*Testily*) As I thought! We haven't another set of mats here. What we have are at the bottom of the linen chest upstairs and they'll simply reek of mothballs.
BASIL (*nervously*) Oh I say, we can't use those.
BARBARA (*snapping*) Of course we can't. (*Returning to the dresser*) We shall have to use a table-cloth. (*She produces a white table-cloth from a drawer, and moves to the table*) It won't look nearly so nice, but it can't be helped. Can I come there now, Delia?

(DELIA *takes her cloth to the kitchen*)

GEORGE (*muttering*) I don't mind a table-cloth.
BARBARA (*witheringly*) I'm sure you're only *saying* that, George—
GEORGE (*eagerly*) No, honestly!

(BARBARA *gives a little whinny as she lays the cloth.* DELIA *returns*)

BARBARA. Delia, the tray, please.

(DELIA *takes the tray from the settee. The telephone rings*)

BASIL (*moving quickly to the telephone*) I'll answer it.

(FAITH BRANTINGHAM *appears from the stairs. She is a luscious-looking creature of about twenty-eight*)

GEORGE. Are you sure there isn't anything I can . . . (*He sees Faith*) Oh, my Lord!

(*The others turn, following* GEORGE'S *startled gaze.* DELIA *backs down* R)

FAITH. Hello, darlings!
BARBARA. Oh!
BASIL (*holding the 'phone well away from his face*) Oh—oh my . . . George! Miss Brantingham!
GEORGE (*quickly*) Leave this to me, old boy. (*He moves up* c)
DELIA (*muttering*) No, don't!
BASIL (*just gaping at Faith; dazedly*) Miss Brantingham!

(BARBARA *moves* L *of the table*)

GEORGE (*with nervous heartiness*) Hello! Come in! Come in! Don't be shy! (*He is about to lead her down*)

(FAITH *sails down* c)

Come and sit down, won't you? (*He dashes to the settee and pats the cushions*)
BARBARA. Are you—are you feeling better now?
BASIL (*still dazedly*) Miss Brantingham!
FAITH (*sitting on the settee*) Thank you.
GEORGE (*coming quickly forward*) Delia, get Miss Brantingham a drink. What's it to be? Gin and tonic. (*To Delia; almost snapping*) Buck up, old girl.

(DELIA *moves* R *and prepares the drink, putting the tray on the drinks cupboard*)

BASIL (*still dazedly*) Miss Brantingham!
GEORGE (*to Faith*) Now you have met everyone, haven't you? This is Barbara and—(*pointing towards Basil*)—and that's Basil. Can't you leave the phone, old boy?
BASIL (*still gaping at Faith*) Phone? (*Realizing he is still holding it*) Oh, God! Excuse me! (*Into the phone*) Hello . . . hello? (*Then turning and looking again; dazedly*) Miss Brantingham!

(DELIA *brings drink above the settee to George, then picks up the tray and moves to the fireplace*)

GEORGE. Oh, thanks. (*About to drink it*) Oh no, of course. (*Handing drink to Faith*) Miss Brantingham.

(FAITH *takes the drink and almost finishes it in one*)

(*As she does this; under his breath*) My God! I mean—can I get you another?

FAITH (*handing him the glass*) I never drink midday!

BASIL (*moving excitedly away from the phone, still holding the receiver*) Miss Brantingham—Miss Brantingham . . .

FAITH. Yes?

BASIL. It's—it's for you?

FAITH (*rising*) Thank you.

(FAITH *moves towards Basil.* BASIL, *in his nervousness, advances towards her, with the result that the phone is dragged off the desk*)

BASIL (*as the phone clatters to the floor*) Aah!

(BASIL *shoves the receiver in* FAITH's *hand and picks up the phone cradle and almost unconsciously stands with it in his hands. While* FAITH *is speaking into the phone* BASIL *is slowly moving in a circle which causes* FAITH *to do the same. Both do this unconsciously*)

FAITH (*into the phone*) Hello . . . Who? . . . *Dar*ling!

(BASIL *gives a big start*)

BARBARA (*hoarsely—to* Faith) You'll excuse me if I . . . (*She indicates "laying" table*)

(FAITH *beams at her*)

BARBARA (*muttering*) Rather pushed for time!

FAITH (*into the phone*) . . . Of course I am, darling! . . . How sweet of you . . . Yes, I'm perfectly all right . . .

(*The rotating has started—*BASIL *with his eyes glued on Faith, goes slowly round. He has to step over the flex as he does this*)

Bless you, of course I am. How did it happen? . . . Oh, some clumsy oaf pushed me in.

(*Looks between the other four*)

(*Into the phone; slowly rotating also*) Did I get what? . . . Roses? What roses? . . . No, I . . .

(GEORGE, *on the mention of roses starts guiltily, then dashes up to the roses, which are sodden with water, picks them up quickly and tears over to Faith with them and thrusts them at her*)

(*Taking them, then realizing they are very wet*) Oh yes, darling, they're here . . . Lovely . . . (*Holding them at arms length and shaking them vigorously*) . . . perfectly lovely!

(GEORGE *wipes his brow and comes down* L *of Delia*)

Bless you. (*She makes kissing noises into the phone*) Darling!

(BARBARA, *almost snorting, picks up a handful of cutlery from Delia's tray, rather noisily*)

GEORGE (*noisily reprimanding her*) Sssssssh!

(DELIA *turns and glares at him*)

FAITH (*into the phone*) What was that? I couldn't quite catch . . . ?
But of *course* I am!

(GEORGE *in his eagerness to get things moving begins taking things
from the tray and putting them on the table*)

BARBARA (*hoarsely, under her breath*) No, George, *no*!

GEORGE (*also hoarsely*) It's all right, Barbara, honestly. (*He picks
up a plate from the tray*)

FAITH (*into the phone*) Whatever made you think I *shouldn't* be?
I'm coming down right away!

GEORGE (*it is a yelp*) What? (*His hand jerks down quickly. The plate
breaks on the edge of the table*)

(BASIL, BARBARA *and* DELIA *all give little yelps and glares at George*)

FAITH (*into the phone*) I'm sorry, darling, I just can't hear. There
seems to be a disturbance—(*She looks towards George*)—somewhere.

GEORGE (*getting on hands and knees, grovelling*) I—I'll pick it up.
But did you hear what she . . . ?

FAITH (*into the phone*) Yes, darling, right away.

BASIL (*still rotating, frantic but timorous*) But, Miss Brantingham . . .

FAITH (*into the phone*) Oh, and Tony darling, would you be a
perfect angel and ask Bessie to get me some sandwiches . . .

(*This is too much for* GEORGE, *he gets to his feet and almost hurls
pieces of broken plate on to tray which* DELIA *is still holding and dashes
up* R *of Faith*)

GEORGE. Sandwiches! Miss Brantingham!

BASIL (*desperately*) Miss Brantingham!

FAITH (*looking irritably at them both, then into the phone*) Oh—er—
smoked salmon, darling. I shan't have time for lunch.

(BARBARA, *who was about to put more things on the table, stops dead
for a moment, then deliberately puts things back on the tray, and during the
following dialogue continues to put things from the table back on to the
tray.* DELIA *gapes at her*)

BASIL. But, Miss Brantingham . . . (*Then as he looks round wildly,
and sees what Barbara is doing*) Babs—darling—no—not yet!

BARBARA (*firmly*) Here and now!

FAITH (*into the phone*) In about twenty minutes, darling.

GEORGE (*almost digging Faith in the ribs*) No, no!

FAITH (*turning and gaping at him*) What?

GEORGE (*shaking his head vigorously*) Not for hours!

FAITH. What on earth are you talking about? (*Into the phone*)
Not you, darling. There's someone here . . . (*to George*) Excuse me.
(*Into the phone*) Bye-bye, my sweet. Twenty minutes! Bless you!

(*She makes kissing noises into the phone, then hands Basil the receiver. Speaking generally*) My leading man. A dreadful clot; can't act for nuts! Hoping for a part in my next play; won't get it, of course!

BASIL (*coping with the phone and flex*) But, Miss Brantingham—George . . . (*He moves to the desk*)

GEORGE (*leading Faith to the settee; wildly*) Miss Brantingham—you're not going—you can't mean you're going *now*.

FAITH. Of course! (*Smiling and taking* c *stage below the settee*) I must!

BASIL (*having put the phone down on the desk, but unconsciously got flex round one foot, coming forward quickly*) But Miss Brantingham . . . ! (*Again the phone is jerked to the floor with a clatter*) Aaaah! (*He returns and unwinds flex and puts the phone back on the desk*)

GEORGE (*gibbering, to Faith*) But you can't—you can't . . . !

FAITH (*gaping*) What?

GEORGE (*indicating the tray*) Lunch—everything's ready . . .

BASIL (*moving above* L *of the settee*) Smoked salmon—chicken—Grand Marnier . . .

FAITH (*smiling "sweetly" at Barbara*) How sweet and what a shame! But really . . .

GEORGE (*almost shouting*) And then after lunch we've got to *talk*.

FAITH (*beaming sweetly on them all*) Bless you. You've all been so terribly sweet. I'd have adored a little chat, but it's quite, quite out of the question. You *do* understand, don't you?

BARBARA. Frankly, no!

FAITH (*with a whoop*) Matinee, darling!

(GEORGE *breaks down* R)

(*Moving up* C) Is there a taxi rank around here?

BASIL (*to* R *of Faith*) At the end of the street, but . . .

FAITH (*preparing for sweeping exit*) Well now . . . Good-bye all!

BARBARA (*heavily*) Good-bye!

FAITH (*suddenly*) Oh! If you would all care to come to the matinee—I should be thrilled to arrange seats for you!

BASIL (*burbling*) Matinee—I—I . . .

FAITH. I'll arrange seats for you, and I'd love to ask you round to my dressing room afterwards, but my agent is coming down to see me—(*Beaming*)—to discuss my new play.

BASIL (*blankly*) Your *new* play?

FAITH. Uh-huh!

GEORGE. You mean you've—*fixed* your new play?

FAITH. This morning—wonderful play—wonderful part. Might have been written for me.

BASIL (*groaning*) Oh!

FAITH (*with a touch of "drama"*) I play the part of a nun!

BASIL (*yelping*) A nun? (*He sits on the back of the settee*)

GEORGE (*yelping*) A—nun!

FAITH (*with great "to-do"*) Ssssh! It's a secret! No one must know yet! It's all terribly "hush-hush"! (*To Basil, as she moves to the hall*) Taxi at the end of the street, did you say?

BASIL (*moving up to the hall*) I—I—I'll see you to the . . .

FAITH. Bless you, darling. (*With a turn and grand wave to the others*) Bye! Bye-bye!

(FAITH *goes, followed by* BASIL. GEORGE *flops on to the settee, stunned*)

BARBARA (*blankly*) A nun! *Her?* With *those* . . . (*She pulls up quickly and coughs embarrassedly*) With that figure! (*She sits above the table*)

GEORGE. And to think that I went to all that trouble—when all the time . . .

BARBARA (*fuming*) *You* went . . . ? And what about me? Slaving over a hot stove on the hottest day we've had this year . . .

DELIA (*sitting L of the table*) And me, run off my feet chasing after the damned woman!

BARBARA. And all for nothing.

GEORGE (*groaning*) Aaah!

DELIA. And poor Basil! What he must be feeling like!

GEORGE (*gaping*) What the devil are you talking about—"poor Basil"?

DELIA. Why, his play—poor lamb—wasn't he hoping that she would do it?

GEORGE (*jumping up*) But, dammit, don't you realize that she . . .

(BASIL *tears back into the room.* GEORGE *sits again*)

BASIL (*rushing R of Barbara*) Babs—darling . . .

BARBARA (*rising; furiously*) Don't speak to me!

BASIL (*excitedly*) What? But, darling . . . !

BARBARA (*fuming*) I said don't speak to me! You've had your fun; you've had your games, and a lot of good it's done you! But now, if you don't mind, we'll all pull ourselves together and try to behave like normal human beings.

BASIL (*gaping at her*) But—Babs . . .

BARBARA (*sweeping on*) Lunch will be ready—on the kitchen table—in fifteen minutes! (*She picks up the tray*)

BASIL. My darling, what does lunch matter?

BARBARA. *What?*

BASIL. *Damn* the lunch!

BARBARA. Basil Mar . . . !

BASIL (*moving excitedly away R*) To hell with lunch! (*To George*) I couldn't eat a bite, could you, George?

GEORGE (*firmly*) Yes—several!

BASIL (*crossing below the table to L of Delia and giving her a hug and a kiss*) Oh, Delia! Isn't it wonderful?

DELIA (*gaping at him*) Basil, what's the matter with . . . ?

BASIL (*sweeping up L of the table to L of Barbara*) My darling . . .

(*He takes the tray from Barbara, plants it on the table, and tries to take her in his arms*)

BARBARA (*disengaging herself from his embrace*) Basil! What are you . . . ? Have you gone mad—eventually?

BASIL (*suddenly seeing red and snapping at her*) For God's sake, Babs! What's the *matter* with you?

BARBARA (*fuming*) Matter—with *me*?

BASIL. Haven't you any—any—*humanity* in you at all?

BARBARA. How dare you . . . ? After all I've been through . . .

BASIL (*flaring*) All right! All right! We *know*! You've had a hell of a morning. Standing over a hot stove. But what the hell? Surely to heaven *this* makes up for everything?

BARBARA (*storming*) What makes up for . . . ?

BASIL. Or are you so eaten up with self-pity that . . .

GEORGE (*stoically*) Steady as she goes, old man!

BARBARA. Basil Martin . . .

BASIL. . . . so eaten up with self-pity that you're going to nurse your—miserable, maggotty, pettifogging little grievance to your bosom and deliberately throw a blight over, what should be the happiest day in your husband's life?

BARBARA (*furious, but also bewildered*) Miserable—maggotty—pettifogging . . . ?

BASIL. All three! (*He rages above the settee to* R)

BARBARA (*unbelievingly*) Ooooh! (*To George and Delia*) You *hear* him? "The happiest day in his life," he says! Just because he's been offered free seats for a matinee! (*She moves up* LC)

BASIL (*stopping dead*) What?

BARBARA. And *he* calls *me* maggotty-minded!

GEORGE (*as before*) Steady as she goes, old girl!

DELIA (*to George; quickly*) Can't you change the record?

BASIL (*moving above the settee and gaping at Barbara unbelievingly*) Seats—for—a—matinee! *Can I believe my ears?*

BARBARA. Ask *them;* not me!

BASIL (*angry, incredulous and deliberate*) Are you telling me that you haven't even grasped the fact that it is *my* play—*your husband's play* that Faith Brantingham is going to do?

BARBARA (*stunned*) *What?*

DELIA (*gaping*) Basil! No!

BASIL (*slowly and in high dudgeon*) Strike—me—poppy colour! (*He stalks* R *of the settee; to the others*) Would you believe—would you credit—my own wife doesn't even recognize my play when it's talked about!

BARBARA (*flattened but trying to keep face*) But—how could I recognize . . .

BASIL (*shouting*) Dammit! (*He moves down* R) You heard her say she was going to play a nun, didn't you? Well, surely . . .

BARBARA. How was I to know there was a nun in it? I've never read the play!

BASIL (*grandly to others, as he strides around*) You hear? (*He crosses to the fireplace*) Out of her own lips! She's never even *read* the play! (*Shouting again*) And why haven't you read the play?

BARBARA (*almost shouting back*) Because you've never *asked* me to!

BASIL (*with a roar*) Asked you to? (*Moving up* L *of the table by the fireplace*) You're my wife, aren't you? I shouldn't *have* to *ask* you! You should have been on your knees—grovelling—panting to read it!

BARBARA (*picking up tray and moving above the settee; seething*) If you will excuse me . . . !

BASIL (*now in full spate, striding to* L *of her*) I will *not* excuse you! You will kindly give me two minutes of your undivided attention! Now! I propose accepting Miss Brantingham's invitation to the matinee this afternoon.

BARBARA. I hope you don't expect me to come with you!

BASIL (*waving a hand airily*) Your presence is a matter of complete indifference to me! George and Delia will accompany me—won't you, George and Delia?

GEORGE (*somewhat flummoxed*) What? Oh! Well I . . . Oh yes, rather!

BASIL. Delia?

DELIA (*also flummoxed*) Well—unless Barbara . . . Are you still going up on the Downs, Barbara?

BARBARA. I most certainly am!

DELIA. Well in that case . . .

BASIL. Then that is settled! But first we shall require lunch.

BARBARA. You just said you couldn't eat a . . .

BASIL. I've changed my mind! Therefore, will you kindly see that lunch is ready in ten minutes from—(*He looks at his wrist-watch, pauses for a moment, then*)—now!

BARBARA. You'll have it in the kitchen.

BASIL. The kitchen—the coalhouse—but we have it in ten minutes!

DELIA. Can—can I help you, Barbara?

BARBARA (*moving, with the tray, to the kitchen, turning and glaring at Basil*) No, thank you, Delia! I must work out my *penance* alone! (*She goes into kitchen and during the ensuing dialogue begins to prepare the table*)

(BASIL *slaps his chest with both hands and strides down* R, *very pleased with himself*)

GEORGE (*eyeing Basil askance*) I say—old man—I don't want to interfere—I mean it's none of my business . . . but don't you think you rather overdid it—going for poor Babs like that?

BASIL (*circling below the settee to above* L *of it*) There comes a day in every man's life, George, when he has to assert himself; that is, if he is to remain worthy of the name of "man"!

GEORGE (*doubtfully*) Yes, I suppose *so*. All the same . . . !

BASIL. Be warned in time, George! (*He moves up* R *of the settee*)

GEORGE (*alarmed*) What? Oh—yes! Yes, rather! (*He turns to Delia and glares fiercely at her. Speaking very patronizingly*) You want to come to the matinee, you say?

DELIA (*somewhat startled*) What? Yes, I suppose . . .

GEORGE. Do you—or don't you? Make up your mind!

DELIA (*snapping*) Of course I'm coming.

GEORGE (*rising and pointing towards the staircase*) Then go and get yourself ready!

DELIA (*gaping at him*) What? I am ready—practically.

GEORGE. Practically is not completely. I suggest you finish the operation.

DELIA. Now look here . . .

GEORGE. For instance—some powder on the nose, and stockings on the legs!

DELIA (*rising*) George Padstow . . . !

GEORGE (*firmly*) I do not like to see my women naked. Well, not at the theatre, anyway!

BASIL (*horrified*) George!

GEORGE (*to Delia*) Beat it! (*He advances on Delia below the table to* L *and backs her towards the hall*)

(DELIA *backs up* C)

DELIA (*furiously*) Now, don't you get the idea that just because Basil thinks he can . . .

(GEORGE *gives a sudden run above the table towards her*)

(*With a squeak*) Aaah! (*Then furiously*) Ooooh!

(DELIA *stamps off up the stairs*)

BASIL (*shocked*) Now really, George . . . !

GEORGE (*as he comes down stage to* L *of the settee, swaggering in the same way that Basil did*) There's something in what you say, old boy! Damn glad you warned me!

BASIL (*moving down* R) Er—yes! (*Suddenly*) I suppose I'd better ring up and order a taxi. We shan't have too much time.

GEORGE. Why a taxi? I've got the car; save the expense.

BASIL. That's very decent of you, old man!

GEORGE. Not at all, old boy. Shall I pop across to the garage for it right away?

BASIL (*after quick look towards the kitchen*) Yes, I'll come with you, old man.

GEORGE (*moving towards the hall*) Fine, old boy! Oh! She may want some petrol . . .

(BASIL *follows to* L *of George*)

BASIL. Petrol? (*Taking out his wallet and checking contents*) Oh! Well, look, old man, you must let me . . .

GEORGE (*half-heartedly*) Good Lord, no, old boy. Wouldn't dream of it.

BASIL. I insist.

GEORGE. Oh—of course, if you insist . . . (*He moves on towards hall*) Come to think of it, she may want some oil too.

BASIL (*following George*) What? Oh! (*Muttering as he goes*) How are the tyres? Want renewing?

(GEORGE *and* BASIL *exit into the hall and off.* BARBARA *leaves the table in the kitchen to inspect the pans on the cooker and look in the oven. She then turns, wipes her brow and returns to the table. There is a knock on the back door*)

BARBARA (*calling*) Come in! (*She moves upstage*)

(*The door opens slowly and the* MILKMAN's *head comes round it.* NOTE: *This scene should be played for charm*)

(*Surprised*) Oh! Milkman—it's you!

(*The* MILKMAN *is very dejected*)

MILKMAN (*cautiously*) Is—is it—all right, ma'am?

BARBARA (*pleased, but a little embarrassed*) All right?

MILKMAN. For me to come in?

BARBARA. Of course.

MILKMAN (*coming into the kitchen somewhat awkwardly*) I mean—I haven't brought any milk or anything . . .

BARBARA (*puzzled and a little anxious*) That's all right. (*She moves above the table*) I wasn't expecting you until—well . . .

MILKMAN. I've just finished work, ma'am. I—I . . . (*After a slight pause; sadly*) I thought I'd better come round and tell you right away, ma'am.

BARBARA (*slight pause*) Tell me—what?

MILKMAN (*unhappily*) Our—run out to the Downs this afternoon, ma'am. I'm sorry, but . . .

BARBARA (*quietly*) Oh! You've come to tell me it's—off. Is that it?

MILKMAN (*moving* R *of her; but a certain distance apart; dejectedly*) Yes, ma'am. I'm sorry . . .

BARBARA (*after a slight pause, bravely*) Oh, well . . .

MILKMAN (*miserably*) Agnes *would* let me down just when . . . (*He tails off miserably*)

BARBARA (*almost sharply*) Agnes?

MILKMAN (*with an apologetic smile*) The scooter, ma'am.

BARBARA (*gaping*) The . . . ?

MILKMAN. Always called her Agnes—don't know why, really.

BARBARA. And how has she let you down?

MILKMAN. She's—conked out.

BARBARA (*flatly*) Oh!

MILKMAN (*woefully*) First time it's happened since I've had her.

She was as right as rain going to work this morning; went like a bird! But when I went to go home on her just now she—she . . .

BARBARA. She conked out.

MILKMAN (*sadly*) Yes, ma'am.

BARBARA. Oh, well . . .

MILKMAN. The engine starts, but she won't go.

BARBARA (*forlornly*) Plenty of petrol?

MILKMAN (*sadly*) Oh yes, ma'am. Filled up last night—and oil. No, it's the rear drive shaft.

BARBARA. The rear drive . . . ?

MILKMAN. Yes, ma'am. You see that's the shaft that transmits the power from the gearbox to the bevelled pinion on the rear axle.

BARBARA. Is it?

MILKMAN. Yes, ma'am, and it's broke. I—I'm sorry, ma'am.

BARBARA (*smiling sadly again*) You couldn't help it. It's not your fault.

MILKMAN. No, ma'am.

BARBARA. It was very kind of you to take the trouble to come and tell me.

MILKMAN (*earnestly*) Oh, I couldn't have just not turned up without letting you know why, could I, ma'am.

BARBARA. No.

MILKMAN (*after a slight, awkward pause*) I came up on a bus.

BARBARA (*with a slight break in her voice*) Did you?

MILKMAN. Yes, ma'am.

(*There is a slight pause*)

BARBARA (*not knowing quite what to say*) Can you get a bus home direct from here?

MILKMAN. No, ma'am. I get a forty-six then change to a twenty-five A.

BARBARA (*hesitantly*) You're going to be terribly late for lunch, aren't you?

MILKMAN. It doesn't matter—now.

(*They have both been standing quite a distance from each other during most of the foregoing dialogue, but are now, quite unconsciously, and very gradually, closing in*)

(*After a rather awkward pause*) Everything—all right with you now, ma'am?

BARBARA. All right? Oh, you mean . . .

MILKMAN. Got over your—your trouble?

BARBARA. Yes—thank you.

MILKMAN. I'm glad. It quite upset me to see you so—upset.

BARBARA. It was very silly of me, really.

MILKMAN. Can't help it now and again, can you? 'S a matter of fact I could have cried nearly when Agnes conked out. I was—sort of—looking forward to . . .

BARBARA (*quite impulsively taking his hand, but almost immediately, on realizing what she has done, letting it drop*) I was too.

MILKMAN (*simply*) Thank you, ma'am.

BARBARA (*with an attempt at lightheartedness*) But there we are; it's just—one of those things. (*After a slight pause, turning away and looking down on the floor; very quietly*) And perhaps it's just as well.

MILKMAN (*quietly*) You know best, ma'am.

(*There is a pause*)

BARBARA. Have you—haven't you got a—girl friend?

MILKMAN (*quite ingenuously*) I suppose I have, really.

BARBARA (*looking up at him, smiling a little*) Don't you know?

MILKMAN. What I mean is—there's no—*understanding*, if you know what I mean.

BARBARA. But you're fond of her?

MILKMAN. She's all right.

BARBARA. You don't sound very . . .

MILKMAN. I haven't known her long. (*After a slight pause*) Mind you, she's not a bad dancer.

BARBARA (*half smile*) Can she *cook*?

MILKMAN (*solemnly*) That's what I've got to find out. If she *can*, well—(*He shrugs his shoulders*)—I might do worse!

BARBARA (*with a little laugh*) And if she can't?

MILKMAN (*also with a little laugh*) She'll get her cards!

(*They both try to laugh*)

(*After a slight pause*) Do *you* like dancing, ma'am?

BARBARA. I *used* to love it.

MILKMAN. *Used* to?

BARBARA (*shaking her head*) I haven't danced for years.

MILKMAN. Oh, what a shame.

BARBARA (*with a wry smile*) I've almost forgotten how . . .

MILKMAN. We have a smashing dance every week at our social club. Not very posh, mind you, but—quiet and—nice, if you know what I mean.

BARBARA (*nodding her head*) H'mm.

MILKMAN. Can't stand the big dance halls these days; too many teenagers yelling all over the place. (*Hopefully*) Wish you could come to one of our dances, ma'am. (*He moves nearer to her*)

BARBARA (*shaking her head*) Wish I could. As I say, I've almost forgotten . . . (*She is in his arms*)

MILKMAN (*quietly*) Nothing to it, ma'am.

(*They begin to waltz slowly. As they do, BARBARA begins to hum "Plaisir d'Amour" softly. After a moment the MILKMAN takes up the humming and, with heads close together they waltz quietly round the kitchen table, humming happily. They move towards the back door, then down R*)

(After a while; quietly, reproachfully) You're a *lovely* dancer, ma'am.
Barbara. You're saying that to be kind.
Milkman. No—honest!

(They continue to dance and hum "Plaisir d'Amour")

Barbara *(softly)* You dance wonderfully.
Milkman *(smiling).* Then we're a pair.

(They dance and hum just a little more, then, gradually slow down, then stop, Barbara to R. There is an embarrassed pause. Still in each others arms, the Milkman shyly kisses Barbara's hair, then they look at one another for a moment, before Barbara moves slowly away above the table)

Barbara *(trying to speak lightly)* I'm supposed to be preparing lunch.
Milkman. Oh, I'm sorry if . . .
Barbara. That's quite all right, but I really ought to get on with it now.
Milkman *(with a half smile)* I expect Mum will play pop with me for being late, when I get home.
Barbara *(quietly)* Then I suppose you ought to . . .
Milkman *(moving to the door; reluctantly)* I suppose I ought. *(He looks at Barbara for a moment; then, quietly)* Well—good morning, ma'am. I *am* sorry—about Agnes—and the Downs.

(Barbara tries to speak, but cannot)

Some other time, perhaps . . . ?

(Barbara looks at him for a moment, then turns away with a little sob)

(Rushing down to her and taking her in his arms) There, there, Mrs Martin.

(He holds her tight and sways)

(After a moment) There, there.
Barbara *(after a slight pause, pulling herself together; determinedly)* I'm all right, really I am. It was just that . . .

(Barbara moves away, sniffs once or twice, then suddenly tries to be matter-of-fact)

Barbara. Oh! The nine and a penny I owe for this week. *(Moving towards the connecting door)* Will you take it now?
Milkman. I'll leave it till Monday if you don't mind, I haven't got my book.
Barbara. Just as you wish.

(The Milkman moves slowly and reluctantly to the back door, then turns)

Milkman. Will you—will you be wanting any extra milk tomorrow, ma'am?

BARBARA. Yes, please—in fact for the next fortnight—two pints extra.

MILKMAN. Every day?

BARBARA. Every day, please.

MILKMAN. Right, ma'am. (*After a pause*) Good afternoon, ma'am.

BARBARA (*standing quite still, looking towards him*) Good afternoon.

(*The* MILKMAN, *after a long look, turns and goes out quickly.* BARBARA *turns, faces front, moves to the table, looks at it for a moment, then putting her hands over her mouth begins to sob quietly.* BASIL *enters from the hall, very perkily. He almost marches into the room, goes towards the kitchen door, stops, frowns, pulls his jacket down very determinedly, then strides to the door, throws it open and marches into the kitchen just as* BARBARA *has begun to cry in earnest*)

BASIL (*firmly and patronizingly*) Well, now! And how are things go— . . . (*He stops dead on seeing Barbara in tears. Horror-stricken*) Babs! (*Almost wildly*) Babs—my darling! (*He rushes to her and sweeps her into his arms. Using exactly the same inflexion and movement as the Milkman*) There, there, my darling! (*Swaying*) There, there!

BARBARA (*sobbing, her downstage hand on his shoulder*) Oooooch!

BASIL. There, there! (*He slips her hand gently round his neck*) There, there! (*He sways her to and fro soothingly, holding her very close*) There, there!

BARBARA. Oh, Basil . . . !

(*They sway for a moment or two*)

BASIL (*brokenly*) Darling, what an utter swine I am.

BARBARA (*brokenly*) You're not! I am! Not reading your play . . .

BASIL (*fervently*) No! *I* am! I am! Slanging you the way I did— in front of George and Delia—and then—sending you in here— leaving you all alone to break your little heart—with not a soul to comfort you!

(BARBARA *draws away a little so that she can look into his face. Having done so, she quickly buries her face in his jacket again and sobs louder than ever*)

BARBARA. Ooooh!

BASIL (*swaying*) There, there, my darling. (*He kisses her hair*)

(*They sway*)

BARBARA (*at last; brokenly*) Lunch!

BASIL. Lunch?

BARBARA. Ten minutes you said.

BASIL. Oh, my sweet! You didn't think I really meant that, did you?

BARBARA (*nodding her head*) Mmmmps! Your matinee . . .

BASIL. To hell with the matinee! I won't go! I'll come up on the Downs with you.

(BARBARA *gives a strangled sob*)

BARBARA. I—I'm not going on the Downs.

BASIL. Not?

BARBARA. NO! (*After a slight pause*) I . . . I want to come to the matinee with you, if . . . (*She looks at him piteously*) If you'll let me!

BASIL. Oh, my dear! (*He hugs her tightly, then kisses her—on the lips this time*)

    (*The front door is heard to slam and* GEORGE's *excited voice is heard calling*)

GEORGE (*off*) Basil! I say! Bas', old boy! . . .

    (GEORGE *comes into the living-room from the hall*)

(*Anxiously*) I say . . . ! (*Looking round*) Where are you old boy? (*He moves above the sofa*)

BASIL (*still hugging Barbara; muttering*) Oh, God! What's wrong now? (*He moves away from her*)

    (DELIA *rushes downstairs and into the room, to* L *of George*)

DELIA (*anxiously*) What are you shouting . . . George, what is it? (*With a wail*) What have you done *this* time?

GEORGE. Where's Basil?

    (BASIL *enters the living-room to* R *of George*)

BASIL. I'm here, George. What's the trouble?

    (BARBARA *now comes into the connecting doorway*)

GEORGE (*quickly, excitedly*) Old Sam Harris!

BASIL (*bewildered*) Old Sam . . . ?

GEORGE (*still quickly and excitedly*) You *remember*—he was at school with us!

BARBARA (*ominously*) What about him?

GEORGE. Just run into him outside—with his wife and kids— asked them in for drinks.

BASIL   } (*together*) {GEORGE!
BARBARA }   {Oh—NO!

Amid consternation from the others, GEORGE *turns blithely to the hall, as—*

the CURTAIN *falls*

FURNITURE AND PROPERTY LIST

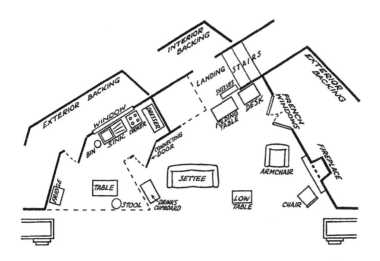

ACT I

On stage: *In living-room:*

Settee (RC). *On it:* cushions, newspapers, empty cigarette cartons, books

Armchair (up LC). *On it:* cushions, papers, magazines

Small chair (down L)

Drinks cupboard and shelves (down R). *On them:* glasses, sherry, whisky, brandy, gin, tonic water, bottle opener

Polished folding table (up C)

Desk (up L). *On it:* writing materials, telephone

Shelves (above desk and table up C). *On them:* vases, ornaments

Coffee-table (below L of settee). *On it:* ashtray (full)

In alcove above fireplace: radio

On mantelpiece: vases, clock, ashtray (full), cigarette-box with one cigarette

On floor and furniture generally: papers, empty bottles, dirty glasses, litter

Carpet

Window curtains (closed)

In kitchen:

Refrigerator (down R). *In it:* sausages, bacon, eggs
Sink and draining-board (up RC). *On board:* soap, towel. *In sink:* bowl. *In cupboard below:* frying-pan, oven dishes, brush and pan, clean towel
Cooker (up RC). *On it:* pans, 2 kettles
Dresser (above connecting door). *On it:* cups, saucers, plates, tea-pot, tea-caddy, sugar-bowl, pastry-board, trays, bowls, bread-bin, cruets, sauce bottles, coffee tin, lemon. *In drawers:* spoons, knives, forks, scissors, table mats, carton of carbolic soap, cake of toilet soap, duster, table-cloth. *In cupboard:* electric iron with base treated to make stain mark
Table (C). *On it:* tray, milk jug
Stool (below table)
Below sink: pedal waste-bin
Above fridge: Hoover cleaner, ironing-board
On wall over fridge: mirror

Off stage: 2 used tea-cups, cigarette end in one, to replace those taken off on tray by Basil (BARBARA)
Letter (BASIL)
Bar of "suddy" carbolic soap, to substitute for unopened carton (DELIA)
Pint bottle of milk (MILKMAN)

Personal: GEORGE: lighter
BARBARA: handkerchief

ACT II

SCENE I

Strike: Everything from kitchen table
Everything from table up C
All dirty dishes and glasses
All newspapers and general untidiness

Set: Cigarette-box back on mantelpiece
Hoover cleaner LC
Small plate on table up C

Check: Room tidy
Ashtrays emptied and replaced

Off stage: 3 blankets (BARBARA)
2 hot-water bottles (BARBARA)

Personal: Pencil and used envelope (BASIL)

ACT II

Scene 2

Strike: Blankets and hot-water bottles

Set: Chair back to down L
On kitchen table: spoons, bowls (mixture in one) whisk, plates, packets of flour, general cooking utensils
On cooker: pans of food
In oven: pans of food
On coffee-table (moved near settee): newspaper spread, silver dishes including small tray and vase, tin of *Silvo*, polishing rags

Off stage: Tray with coffee cup and saucer, pot, cream jug, spoon (DELIA)
Basket with smoked salmon, olives, cocktail biscuits, 2 bottles of Graves, ½ bottle of Grand Marnier (BASIL)
Suitcase (DELIA)
Dress (DELIA)
2 pint bottles of milk (MILKMAN)

ACT III

Strike: Coffee-table
Polishing materials
Iron
Ironing-board

Set: Bottles and glasses on display on drinks cupboard
Table from up C opened out and down LC. *On it:* places set for 5 people, 5 small plates, 5 large knives, 5 small knives, 5 spoons, 5 large forks, 5 small forks, 5 mats, silver cruets, bread basket, caster, table napkins, various glasses, etc.
5 small chairs round table
Rug over burnt patch in carpet
Script on settee
Silver vase on shelves C
Large tray by kitchen dresser
Swab cloth in sink
Tea-cloth under sink

Check: Pans on cooker and in oven
Kitchen table tidied up

Off stage: Tray with empty glass and tonic-water bottle (DEL)
Bunch of roses with card (BASIL)

Personal: GEORGE: watch
BASIL: wallet

LIGHTING PLOT

Property fittings required: pendants, wall brackets (none practical)

INTERIOR. A living-room and kitchen. The same scene throughout

THE APPARENT SOURCES OF LIGHT are windows up RC in the kitchen and up L in the living-room

THE MAIN ACTING AREAS are up R, RC, up C, down C, LC, up L

ACT I. Morning

To open: Full daylight in kitchen, living-room dim

Cue 1   BARBARA opens living-room curtains   (Page 1)
Bring up living-room lighting to full

ACT II. SCENE 1. Morning

To open: As close of previous act
No cues

ACT II. SCENE 2. Morning

To open: As close of previous scene
No cues

ACT III. Midday

To open: As close of previous act
No cues

EFFECTS PLOT

ACT I

Cue 1	BARBARA shakes cushions *Kettle whistles*	(Page 1)
Cue 2	BASIL exits *Running water*	(Page 7)
Cue 3	GEORGE: "I know the kind" *Jet of water hits kitchen doorstep*	(Page 10)
Cue 4	GEORGE: " . . . saying, Bas old boy?" *Doorbell rings*	(Page 19)

ACT II

SCENE 1

Cue 5	After CURTAIN up *Telephone rings*	(Page 30)
Cue 6	BARBARA switches on radio *Dance band plays "Plaisir d'Amour"*	(Page 30)
Cue 7	BARBARA switches off radio *Music off*	(Page 30)
Cue 8	BASIL: "Gordon Pirie?" *Telephone rings*	(Page 35)
Cue 9	BASIL picks up kettles in kitchen *Doorbell rings*	(Page 37)
Cue 10	BARBARA: " . . . put me away" *Doorbell rings*	(Page 41)
Cue 11	BASIL: "Bubbles" *Doorbell rings*	(Page 41)
Cue 12	BARBARA: " . . . saying my home . . . " *Doorbell rings*	(Page 42)

ACT II

SCENE 2

Cue 13	DELIA: "Barbara . . . " *Doorbell rings*	(Page 44)
Cue 14	BARBARA: "That's all you need" *Doorbell rings*	(Page 44)
Cue 15	BASIL: " . . . next time, and like it" *Telephone rings*	(Page 49)

ACT III

Cue 16	BARBARA: " . . . fall by the wayside!" *Doorbell rings*	(Page 65)
Cue 17	BASIL: "But . . . " *Doorbell rings*	(Page 65)
Cue 18	BARBARA: "The tray, please" *Telephone rings*	(Page 70)